THIS IS WHO I AM

of related interest

Women and Girls with Autism Spectrum Disorder
Understanding Life Experiences from Early Childhood to Old Age
Sarah Hendrickx
Foreword by Judith Gould
ISBN 978 1 84905 547 5
eISBN 978 0 85700 982 1

Spectrum Women
Walking to the Beat of Autism
Edited by Barb Cook and Dr Michelle Garnet
Foreword by Lisa Morgan
ISBN 978 1 78592 434 7
eISBN 978 1 78450 806 7

Girls with Autism Becoming Women
Heather Stone Wodis
Foreword by Erika Hammerschmidt
ISBN 978 1 78592 818 5
eISBN 978 1 78450 907 1

Life on the Autism Spectrum
A Guide for Girls and Women
Karen McKibbin
Foreword by Tony Attwood
ISBN 978 1 84905 747 9
eISBN 978 1 78450 193 8

THIS IS WHO I AM

The Autistic Woman's Creative Guide to Belonging

ANDREA ANDERSON

Jessica Kingsley Publishers
London and Philadelphia

First published in Great Britain in 2024 Jessica Kingsley Publishers
An imprint of John Murray Press

1

Copyright © Andrea Anderson 2024

The right of Andrea Anderson to be identified as the Author of the Work has been asserted by them in accordance with the Copyright, Designs and Patents Act 1988.

Front cover image source: Caroline Lindop and Jim Burke.

A CIP catalogue record for this title is available from the British Library and the Library of Congress

ISBN 978 1 80501 015 9
eISBN 978 1 80501 016 6

Printed and bound in Great Britain by Bell & Bain Limited

Jessica Kingsley Publishers' policy is to use papers that are natural, renewable and recyclable products and made from wood grown in sustainable forests. The logging and manufacturing processes are expected to conform to the environmental regulations of the country of origin.

Jessica Kingsley Publishers
Carmelite House
50 Victoria Embankment
London EC4Y 0DZ

www.jkp.com

John Murray Press
Part of Hodder & Stoughton Ltd
An Hachette Company

CONTENTS

Part 3: Accepting You're Autistic

Part 4: Belonging

ACKNOWLEDGEMENTS

For Finn and Jake, thank you for all you teach me about the joy of being different. You are both the light of my life.

Lovely Jason... thanks for making me feel safe to be myself. Your encouragement and support means the world.

To all you 'funny' humans, discovering what makes you wonderfully different, truth and liberation awaits you.

To all the wise women and guides who have helped me to find my writing voice and the courage to step forward and challenge for change. Annabel, Selina, Elaine and Zakee, to name but a few.

To all the lovely people who have encouraged me, offered wisdom and celebrated with me in writing this book and getting it published: Emma, Sarah, Silvia, Sarah Lou, Caroline, Amy, Marco, Renata, Kathryn and Murray.

Rachel, the conversation we had about how important it is for children to have an understanding about their differences had a profound effect on me. I am so grateful to you for that.

To my lovely mum and dad, to whom I think I am something of an enigma! Ever experimental and in search of answers. Thanks for opening your mind to my twists and turns.

To all the wonderful people who I make meaningful connections with in the neurodivergent community, thank you. To all the women who get in touch with me, those deep shared exchanges in private corners of social media fill me with joy and a sense of belonging.

To all the fighters in the SEND parent communities. I appreciate all the information and support we give to each other.

Sam K of DJS, you are trailblazing how mainstream education can be an inclusive environment for all children.

Finally... I think I might live in the Capital of Neurodivergence in the UK... Brilliant Brighton! A magnet for alternative thinkers, colourful characters and justice seekers, a place I am happy to call home.

INTRODUCTION

Funny Girl!

I'm Andrea. I lived a life unaware of my autism until my mid-40s. I didn't grow up with any stories of autistic girls or women and I didn't see any autistic women in my books or on my TV screens.

I didn't know that other people found it hard to fit or understand the behaviour that was expected from them in social situations. I didn't realize that other people felt alone in their feelings of otherness – a feeling of being a bit different to everyone else but not really understanding what the difference is.

It took becoming a mum to a wonderful boy who is joyous in his difference and the eventual diagnosis of his autism for me to discover my own autism.

This means I lived a large part of my life not knowing something crucial to my self-understanding and identity.

I want to change that. I want the next generation to see and hear many stories of autistic women and girls. I want the next neurodivergent generation to know they are not alone, they are not wrong and they do not need to hide themselves from the world.

'You're such a funny girl,' my mum would affectionately say to me. From a very young age, I have memories of her saying this. She still says it to me occasionally!

What does she mean? I would think to myself. Why am I a funny girl? At the same time, I could sense there was something different about me but I didn't know what it was that made me different.

She would say it to me when I was sharing worries, of which

I had a *lot*. How was I going to join in with an activity? What was I going to say? What might happen at the social event? Or when I was complaining about how *loud* my brother was! Or how an item of clothing felt – it was too itchy or the label would dig in or it felt weird... patterned tights, anyone? With cut- out bits on them... oh God the texture of those tights!

'Funny' things continue to be part of my life today. In fact, I experienced one when I was reading a story to one of my sons the other night.

The story was called 'The Obvious Elephant'. It describes how some very ignorant villagers do not know what an elephant is, but they ignore the child in the story who does know. They poke and prod the elephant to work out its nature and generally do some quite cruel things to it. Eventually, they listen to the child and accept that the elephant is an elephant (even though a professor tries to take credit for the discovery!). Whilst the child in this story is very clever, he does go on to name the elephant 'One Hundred Per Cent Cotton' because that's what it says on the label of his handkerchief.

The funny thing was not my reading the story – although its relevance to how autistic people are treated was not lost on me! The funny thing was that every time I had to read the words 'One Hundred Per Cent Cotton', this disgusted me in ways I find difficult to explain. I will, however, try...

Synaesthesia, which is when you experience one of your senses through another, is common in autistic folk, and I have a version of it too. Having heightened senses, which affects my sensory processing, coupled with what I think is easiest to explain as a very vivid visual imagination, means that the phrase 'One Hundred Per Cent Cotton' made me imagine how that handkerchief would feel in my mouth – and the mere thought of it set my teeth on edge!

Swiftly moving on from the elephant story, being a Funny Girl with funny ways of seeing, experiencing and communicating with the world was something that plagued me and robbed me of confidence.

When I was growing up, in the 1970s and 80s, this was met with comments such as, 'She's such a worrier' and, in the 90s and 2000s, with, 'She should try harder to manage her stress levels,' but someone like me would be recognized today as an individual who has high-level anxiety, most of which was internalized.

I eventually became confident in my 40s, after having done a great deal of 'work' on myself (in the form of therapy) and been a lifelong learner of how to communicate with confidence. Comfortable in my own skin and a professional coach, being a creative source for transformational change, finally, I knew who I was... ha! Or so I thought!

At the age of 45, one month before a global pandemic, I read the words that were going to change my life and reveal who I truly am! To reveal why some things drain the life from me and why I find groups of people such a challenge, even though I *love* people, to explain why my direct communication can take people's breath away (sorry husband, that mostly applies to you!).

Finally, after five years of being frightened of the inference that my eldest child was autistic and the 'A word' being a whisper in our household, I read about autism and I realized autism lives in me. Since that day, I have been doing quite a dance between my awareness of autism, reviewing my entire life through a new lens, and my acceptance of it.

I am an autistic woman.

This book is written to inform and inspire you. If you're doing your own dance between your awareness and acceptance of autism, then come with me, I will be your guide. I will share with you my lived experience of what has helped me along the way from awareness to acceptance of being autistic.

This book is designed to help you to navigate your own late-life autism discovery. It's full of resources, tools and activities to help you progress from a place of curiosity about what autism means to you, to exploring it more deeply in the strengths your autism gives you, the challenges it can present and what you need to support you with those challenges.

I will be asking you some questions in the form of journal

prompts and giving you activities that will help you to open up new perspectives about yourself. If you want to engage those whom you love in part of these explorations, there are activities that will help you to open up those conversations.

I will take you from the very first clues of my child's autism, my resistance to exploring it, my ignorance of what autism is and the genetic links that exist in neurodivergence. I am candid about my fear, shame and limiting ableist beliefs. I think this is what holds many of us back from a deeper understanding about neurodivergence, and a big part of changing the conversation about autism is to be honest and curious about our individual and collective limiting beliefs.

This book also explores other triggers for us in discovering our autism later in life.

Each chapter will give you an insight from my lived experience, or that of other autists in the chapter, that explores triggers of autism discovery. Then it's over to you to consider how those experiences relate to, or differ from, you and your experiences.

That's often the autist's way of relating to others: someone shares a story and then we may add our own story to that. We do this to show we have understood what they are sharing and can relate to their experience by sharing ours. This can often be misunderstood and misconstrued as us trying to turn the conversation to us, taking attention away from the original storyteller!

We're free from the constraints of social rules here in this book! This is your book of discovery, free from expectations that you will be anything other than someone exploring how being wired differently might affect the way you experience and live in the world.

The book follows a timeline of what naturally unravels when you make the connections and discover your own autism. It explores the difficult emotions you might navigate, along with the practical considerations to be aware of from discovery to diagnosis – if that is a route you are considering.

I will guide you through the reactions you can receive when sharing your autism with others.

Self-awareness is a huge part of accepting autism as part of your identity and accepting yourself as being autistic. The questions and activities in this book are designed to help you do exactly that – accept and celebrate yourself as autistic.

It's challenging for autistic folk to navigate methods of communicating and interacting in ways that are unnatural to us; part of this book helps you to consider how you can best take care of yourself and manage and protect your energy.

The later part of this book explores the external support you might find within the autistic and neurodivergent community.

The final part of this book explores belonging. Feeling safe to belong as an autist – both to yourself and within groups and communities with whom you feel safe to be your authentic autistic self. We'll also explore the changes that need to be implemented for all autists to be fully accepted with all of our different strengths and needs. I invite you to consider the changes you would like to happen for autism to be understood and embraced in all areas of society.

When we all get curious and welcoming of everyone's differences, it makes more inclusive and productive environments for all of us.

You can find out more about the author Andrea Anderson and her work, or contact her, through her website www.who-iam.co.uk.

HOW TO WORK
WITH THIS BOOK

Newly Discovered Autism

If your own late-life autism discovery was recent, read through each chapter, and consider and engage with the question prompts and activities. This book is designed to help you as you go through your own personal process from awareness to acceptance.

Go gently with yourself throughout all of your autism discovery, for it is a major thing to uncover later in life.

Some of you might step into this new identity with what seems like open arms and full enthusiasm. Some of you will be riddled with fear and self-doubt; you may get tangled up in questions and it might become overwhelming at times. You might need to walk away from exploring this, take a break and come back when you feel ready.

From my own experience, even once you get to autistic self-acceptance, the exploration will continue. There is no finish line and I encourage you to find a pace that works best for you.

Say No!

If, like me, you have spent your entire life complying, working incredibly hard to please others and moulding yourself to fit, I wholeheartedly invite you to use this book as a space to say *no*!

To push back on what you're averse to doing – do not force yourself to work though things or to explore questions and activities if you have no enthusiasm for them.

When I coach people to really embrace and accept their authentic selves, to accept their natural strengths and to consider their struggles with compassion – to move towards living in a way they are longing to – I invite them to choose 'yes', 'no' or 'counter offer' in response my requests for them to take a certain action.

I invite you to do the same. Read and work through this book with an open heart and curiosity, and follow your natural enthusiasm.

Push back when your instinct is telling you, 'No, not that!' If there's still curiosity about the part you're reading, pursue with action in a way that works for you, for example, 'I might try this bit out though,' or 'This alternative action will work better for me.'

Revisiting Your Autism Discovery

If you're further down the line with processing your own late-life autism discovery, you may wish to dip in and out of the reflections and activities that may help you to further acknowledge, understand and embrace your autism.

Supporting a Loved One Through Their Autism Discovery

If you have a family member or loved one going through their own process of late-life autism discovery, reading this book cover to cover will give you an insight into what autism is and how it can present, along with helping you to become aware of what they might be experiencing as they grapple with accepting this huge change in how they understand themselves.

Considering the reflection questions will give you a greater appreciation of how you can support them and be an ally to them and the autistic community.

You may be a family member of a late-life discovered autist who recognizes your own autistic traits from reading Chapter 1. In which case, congratulations! Read on and complete your own reflections to help you delve deeper into this discovery.

I Am Not an Expert!

I was very late to the autism party. I was very late in becoming a parent. It was through one of my wonderful children, by becoming aware of his autism, that I discovered my own.

I am not an expert in autism (we need a *lot* more of those, for sure!). What I share with you in this book is from my lived experience of autism before, during and after my journey from awareness to acceptance. I very much wanted to write a book to inform and inspire others about autism. To share what helped me personally and what I hope will help you too.

As a professional coach, I have a lot of tools to help people reach self-acceptance and to provide new perspectives, new possibilities. I bring this experience into this book.

A Quick Guide to the Symbols

	This symbol is a prompt for you to pause and reflect upon what's coming up for you, to let the prompt provoke thought and reflection in you. There's space to jot down a few words, but you can also write down longer reflections in your journal, favourite notebook or elsewhere if you'd like to.
	This symbol is an activity or action prompt. It's inviting you to work through an activity that will deepen your learning and progress you towards self-acceptance.
	This symbol is a prompt for you to pause for a bit of self-compassion, to acknowledge and celebrate what you're working through and how that will help you grow in self-acceptance.

There is still a great deal that is misunderstood about autism. I was very ignorant about autism myself until 2020.

It was a big year for all of us: worldwide, the pandemic meant we were turning on an axis that felt strange and frightening. It was a year of revelations for me and my family. And it was the year I finally welcomed autism into my life and into our family's life.

Feeling stuck and isolated can be a frightening and lonely place to be. Late-life discovery of a huge difference in yourself requires you to go through a process of letting go of old beliefs, old stories and pain. It will bring relief and fear to the surface.

This book will give you the information, tools and resources to navigate that process and it will help you to get to a more liberating place of acceptance – of all that you are and all that's possible for you.

I hope it will lead you to finding belonging. I hope you find your inspirational community and knowledge that so many other folk, all over the world, are getting from awareness to acceptance of their neurodivergence.

If more of us late-life discovered autists share our stories from our lived experience and join in with the conversation of what autism is and how it can present, we are more likely to improve the perception and understanding of autism.

I now know there is much to be celebrated about autism and all that it gives. I would love autistic people of the next generation and beyond to have an entirely different experience, a much more positive experience of it from childhood through to adulthood.

Much needs to change in the areas of health, education and law concerning awareness, understanding and support for neurodivergent people.

This needs to be accessible to *all*, and as a priority to those who need it most. Until this happens, I hope this book will help you find your way.

Part 1

GETTING STARTED

CHAPTER 1

THIS IS AUTISM: THE BASICS

When you've met one person with autism, you've met one person with autism!

Autism is a neurological condition. It is not an illness. It is a spectrum.

Autism affects how people take in information through their senses and how they interpret information, communicate and socialize or interact in groups. It creates differences in how people learn, experience the world and engage with it.

The amount of learning difference or support needed by an autistic person varies widely, hence the reference to a spectrum.

There are many definitions of autism. Many of them are written with a psychological slant and jargon. These definitions can be hard to grasp or relate to.

In line with the purpose of this book, I intend to share with you my lived experience of autism, thereby offering an account of how autism might be experienced.

That's the focus of this chapter – the basics of autism. It will give you a straightforward way to consider how autism relates to you or someone who matters to you.

Further reading and resources are also provided at the end of this book.

Sensory Processing

Autism can affect a person's senses relating to sight, sounds, smell, touch and movement.

These senses can either be over or under sensitive. If an autistic person is particularly heightened to a sense, they may *avoid* whatever is triggering to that sense. If the sense is under sensitive, they may actively *seek out* something that will activate it.

With all sensory processing there will be a tolerance level. Tolerance levels can vary hugely and may depend on factors such as sleep or stress levels.

A day-to-day activity may be tolerated well one day, but another day it might be overwhelming. For example, I am sensitive to sound and movement. A crowded environment or a noisy playground can overwhelm my senses. I find certain smells harder to tolerate, such as those of perfume or fish, but my tolerance levels for smell are slightly higher than my tolerance levels for sound. I find traffic noise or motor noise particularly challenging.

However, I am not sensitive to all sounds. I *love* music and this offers me a lot of sensory soothing. When I can put my headphones on and listen to music, this acts as an excellent way to soothe any potential overwhelm. Likewise, nature acts in much the same way. If I am surrounded by trees or can hear birds, this can soothe the other noises away.

I can navigate a busy room full of chatter, but it will require a lot of energy.

Are you aware of any of your senses that are heightened? Which ones?

. . . .

. . . .

The key point to make here is this: autistic people experience differences with how their senses process. Tolerance levels vary by person and, as mentioned, day-to-day factors play a part, such as how much rest someone has had, their levels of hunger, thirst and wellbeing, etc. Autistic people can mostly navigate these factors but it will take them more energy to do so.

When tolerance levels are exceeded, this can lead to overwhelm, which can have a huge impact on our nervous systems.

When tolerance levels are exceeded on a regular basis, this can lead to autistic meltdowns or autistic shutdowns.

When these tolerance levels are consistently exceeded over time, without any recovery periods or enough rest, this will lead to burnout, affect mental wellbeing and may lead to mental illness.

When there is a lack of awareness, understanding or willingness to adapt environments or the expectations that are placed on an autistic person, this in itself will create additional guilt, shame and stress, all of which can have damaging effects on an autistic person's mental wellbeing and health.

On the flipside of this, if an autistic person can create, or have help in creating, the right environment for them to process their senses, this will allow them to thrive and share with the world the many interesting perspectives that their senses give them.

For me personally, my autism gives me the most wonderful visual images, references and connections. Body movement shifts my energy and gives me great insight into emotions, feelings and possibilities.

Today, I use my senses to help me in my work as a creative coach. For example, I will ask my clients questions about how they imagine their possibility or idea looks, and whether they can see an image, a symbol or a metaphor for it. I may ask what texture or colour it has and about the light around it, and I sometimes even ask them to imagine how it smells! I also ask clients to move and connect with how something feels in their body, to shift their energy from sitting to standing, which in turn shifts their connection and the possibilities open to them.

Using the senses to connect with, describe and make sense

of the world, or the world you want to create, is one of the ways I use my autism to help people use their senses in a creative way.

Communication

The second thing that autism affects is how we communicate.

Some autistic people are nonspeaking. That doesn't mean they don't hear or understand what is going on. They may use writing, drawing, pictures or visual prompts rather than speech to communicate responses or share thoughts and ideas.

Those who do communicate verbally cannot always read the communication cues around timing, content, duration, volume of voice or engagement.

It can be very difficult for autistic people to read the audience. They may have something they are bursting to say, something related to their focused interest or something they desperately want to add, as a way to join in with the conversation. Such may be their enthusiasm or nerves that they mistime it and end up broadcasting information that is not received in the way it is intended!

Much of communication is tied up in body language or eye contact, which can be unreadable for autistic folk. In fact, eye contact can be very difficult full stop, which can lead to much misunderstanding. Socially and culturally, there all sorts of assumptions about people who can't make eye contact, such as their intention, honesty and politeness... the list goes on.

Communication takes up a lot of energy for autistic folk. Not least because a lot of communication has to be dressed up in all sorts of social rules that do not come naturally... small talk can be torturous!

It surprises me, given our society's fixation on efficiency, that the neurotypical world still doesn't value the directness of autistic communication! A neurotypical person's natural perception when met with a direct autistic request or response is, 'They are so rude,' or 'It's just so inappropriate!'

It doesn't come naturally to the autistic mind to dress up the communication or tone it down. Yet in order to be listened to, to be included, to get an opportunity to be heard, that's what we are expected to do.

Which can be exhausting.

I have made it my business to observe and tune into how groups of people communicate, the words they use and the humour that might be used to defuse any heat in conflict. How to engage attention in topics they are most interested in. This was initially a survival technique – to observe, understand how to fit in and then adapt myself to be like them – for the door to be opened.

This astute observation went on to help me in my work in understanding how groups can better communicate and how to make the invisible norms – for example, culture – more visible, to align a business behind a common purpose and set of values.

I am also interested in words – how they sound, how people feel their meaning and the trends in using them; I am endlessly curious about new words adopted by people to show their tribal identity. I have learned not to mimic these words or use them too early when meeting a new group. You must be accepted before using the group dialect to show your tribal identity... use it too soon or too publicly and you face ridicule.

Not all autistic people are interested in or able to observe the invisible nuanced communication cues. This can lead to frustration, for them and for others, and to many misunderstandings and assumptions. To create environments for autistic people to thrive, there needs to be space for curiosity and questions for both autistic and non-autistic, also known as allistic, people.

When I start working with a new coaching client, we design our relationship. We agree what we will both bring, give and get. I invite them to share what might frustrate them and to share with me when something isn't working or when we need to redesign how we work.

Imagine if we could all do that! What if we all designed our relationships? If we honestly shared our needs and our triggers for conflict and agreed how to treat each other when times are tough.

Imagine if we could all design how we communicate with each other.

What's your preferred way to communicate?

. . . .

. . . .

What frustrates you in communication with others?

. . . .

. . . .

What do you bring to relationships in how you communicate?

. . . .

. . . .

How would you like people to communicate with you when times are tough?

. . . .

. . . .

Social Interaction

This is the area, for me, that is the most challenging of all!

Interacting in groups is fraught with danger as an autistic woman. It feels like navigating a minefield. Watching those knowing looks being exchanged in a group and only being able to second-guess what they mean. Being plagued by them. What did those looks mean? What did I do to trigger them? I know I've made a mistake.

Was it what I said, or how I said it?

Take the invisible cues in communication, eye contact, body language and dynamics between people in the group, add in the volume of many people talking and moving about, and then you've got the sensory processing tolerance challenges on top of it all.

I am exhausted just thinking about it!

The other challenge is when people say one thing and then do another. And the complicated dynamics that may exist in the group and the activity that happens outside of it. For example, someone may have confided in you that they find X in the group very challenging and they don't like them. Yet their behaviour towards X does not match that description, either in this social setting or in any activity that happens outside of it.

Whilst I think I have a good grasp of the spectrum of emotions that one may feel, there are some that just do not make it onto my radar. Jealously being a classic example that I just can't grasp. I am honest. I am open. I see the best in people. If I say I will do something, I do it. I am not claiming to be a model citizen. Far from it! But there is an honesty and purity in perception that comes with autism.

Given the right trusting relationships and an open and safe environment, there is little danger in honesty and trust. However, in a highly competitive environment, these traits may be seen as naive and can lead to outcomes that the autistic person would never naturally predict.

What do you find challenging about groups?

. . . .

. . . .

Are there particular groups that you find more challenging than others?

. . . .

. . . .

Which groups do you feel safe in? What distinguishes them from the groups your find challenging?

· ·

· ·

What questions do you have about autism?

· ·

· ·

This Is How I Relate to Autism

The following is designed to get you to consider how your senses process differently. With regard to your senses, consider and write down the things you seek out or take comfort in and the things you find uncomfortable and avoid.

For autistic people these things can be clues to being dysregulated. You may have stronger reactions to the things that you find uncomfortable to process and be around when dysregulated. The things that offer comfort and that you actively seek out can act as a way to soothe your senses when you are dysregulated.

Sense	I seek out	I avoid
Sight/Visual For example: · bright lights · vivid colour · being in crowded/ busy places · fast moving images (TV/film)		
Touch For example: · uncomfortable with certain fabrics/labels · certain food textures · being barefoot · having back rubbed		
Taste/Smell For example: · smelling flowers · perfume · familiar food · adding spice or strong flavours		

cont.

Sense	I seek out	I avoid
Movement For example: · heights · dancing · fast movement · travelling in a car		
Sound For example: · machinery · traffic noise · noise from a crowd · loud music		

SENSORY PROCESSING

Start to note what you can relate to and what you're curious to explore further in relation to your sensory processing:

. . . .

. . . .

. . . .

. . . .

. . . .

. . . .

. . . .

. . . .

. . . .

. . . .

. . . .

. . . .

. . . .

. . . .

. . . .

. . . .

. . . .

. . . .

. . . .

. . . .

. . . .

COMMUNICATION

	Yes	No
I can be very direct in how I communicate, especially when I feel overwhelmed or tired		
I'm so focused on trying to share my point, I struggle to listen to others		
I find eye contact makes me deeply uncomfortable and self-conscious		
I often miss the chance to add my thoughts or points – the conversation has moved on before I get the chance		
I want to get straight to the point and focus on what I need to get from the conversation; I find the small talk and skirting around the crux of the matter pointless and draining		
I prefer to look up when I'm talking; it helps me to focus and I can visualize my thoughts in my head when I do this		
People tell me I'm too much or talk too much about things I'm interested in		
I find eye contact very intensive and distracting from what I'm trying to say		

Other challenges I find with communication are:

. . . .

. . . .

. . . .

. . . .

. . . .

. . . .

. . . .

SOCIAL INTERACTION

	Yes	No
I find it really difficult to understand social cues, especially with a group of people I don't know		
I find endless 'banter' and back-and-forth jokes bewildering and pointless		
I find small talk painful! I understand it's necessary as a warmup; I'd much prefer to talk about things that matter		
I often spend hours consumed with worry about what I will talk about at social events, especially when I don't know many people there		
I often see people exchange glances at each other in group situations; I don't know what these glances mean, but I feel like I've done something wrong		
I often feel exhausted after being around groups of people		
The thought of running out of things to talk about in a group is torturous to me		
Having to talk to different people or be in lots of meetings or group discussions is exhausting for me		

Other challenges I find with social interaction are:

. . . .

. . . .

. . . .

. . . .

. . . .

. . . .

. . . .

If this is the first time you've actively considered how autism relates to you or someone who matters to you, well done for taking a step towards seeing yourself or a person that you care for from a different perspective.

I have purposely made these descriptions and activities on considering autism simple and straightforward.

Discovering yourself as a late-life autist doesn't change the person you are; the essence of your values will still be the same.

Simply put, you will have new information about yourself – about why you see and experience things differently. And you can start to consider the impact those differences may have on you.

As you progress through your explanation of what autism means for you, it might not feel simple as you unravel the layers further and consider your life through an autism lens.

Feel free to revisit this simple explanation of a different way of being and connecting with the world when you need a reminder that you're the same person; now you have new information about how you experience and connect with the world.

Well done for taking a step towards seeing things in a different light.

CHAPTER 2

YOUR DISCOVERY DEAL

Exploring your past, present and potential future through a completely new lens is difficult.

What will follow will feel illogical! Surprising thoughts and emotions will surface as forgotten memories arise.

In this chapter the focus is on an activity to help you bring some of your blocks to deeper discovery to the surface.

We all have positive and negative aspects of our mind. The negative aspects of our mind are designed to illuminate risk and alert us to potential danger. When we allow this part of our mind to be the dominant force, it can limit us and prevent us from progressing. It can paralyze us and keep us stuck.

Unless you've lived a trouble-free life, it can be painful to face old horrors, and embarrassing and shameful experiences. If you're an autist with an acute memory and recall for all the glorious details, it can feel like you're reliving that embarrassment, shame and trauma all over again.

Is it any wonder that your mind will want to find escape routes from this? It will humph and loudly exclaim, 'This is ridiculous! What's the point of dredging this old stuff up?!'

'It's total bollocks! Is autism even a thing?!'

'We're perfectly happy as we are, let's not spoil that, let's not do this – looking at this autism thing.'

And then in its desperation to avoid any discomfort at all, the critical part of that wonderful mind of yours will go for total aggressive avoidance, 'It's all just a hot topic right now, it'll get called out for what it is, don't fall for it... It's bullshit!'

Here's the thing: looking at all those painful memories again, it will be hard, and you'll be equipped with new information about why those things happened.

You'll have new information about what it is that makes you different, you'll know why you approach situations and life differently, why you find some things so difficult and quite a lot of things easy.

Through this, you'll develop a new level of self-understanding, you'll see your strengths in a new light and, quite possibly the most important thing in all of this, you'll develop compassion for yourself and your own needs.

Before you start really delving into exploring you and autism, before you deepen your understanding of how autism shows up in you and in your life, let's clear some space.

Let's suspend disbelief for 30 minutes or so of your life to look at stuff that might be getting in the way. Let's illuminate the heavy stuff, bring it forward in your consciousness to shift it a bit.

For once, it's out of your mind and on the paper, it'll make the autism exploring that's going to be happening for you a bit lighter.

The Artist's Way

When I was pushing this book towards a pathway for publication, I was part of a group following The Artist's Way – the multimillion-copy worldwide bestseller book and course by Julia Cameron.

For I had to push through a lot of noise, self-criticism and self-sabotage that was getting in the way of me believing in this book enough to pitch it to *the* publisher – Jessica Kingsley Publishers!

The following activity is inspired by some tasks Julia Cameron designed to help artists recover a sense of compassion, in particular blasting through the blocks, the things that are in the way of your progression. A couple of these tasks have stuck with me; they helped to really push me forward.

They cleared some space in my mind and minimized the risks of stepping up and pushing myself into the unknown. They also crystallized the changes I wanted to make, the commitment and responsibility I was taking to the changes I wanted to happen.

The Discovery Deal

Resentment and fear can cripple us and prevent us from moving forward.

You're probably going to resent this book... good! It's here to provoke thought, illuminate discomfort and connect you with your strengths – things that are unique to you.

Working though this book, in the way that works for you, will create movement and progression in your awareness of your autism and ultimately acceptance of yourself as autistic.

It will require commitment, action and effort from you. This book will give you the information and tools – the rest is up to you.

Why bother? What's the payoff?! A deeper understanding of and compassion for your needs. A claiming of what autism gives you – for it does give you a unique way of seeing the world; many of your strengths will come from this.

Progressing through your discovery of your autism, getting to a place where you accept yourself as autistic, will give you liberation from the need to fit a mould that wasn't meant for you. A freedom from conformity.

FEAR AND RESENTMENT

List the things you resent about autism, the possibility of being autistic and anything else autism and resentment of it brings up for you. You might be pissed off that there's even a 'thing' that you're having to explore about yourself... 'I don't want to have a thing that makes me different! I want to be the same.'

List your fears about autism – real or projected. What fears do you have about exploring autism, about accepting it, about sharing it? What might it mean for you? What might it change in your life, now or in the future, for you or for others in your life?

Resentment	Fear

What strikes you about your fears? How likely are these fears to become a reality?

. . . .

. . . .

What strikes you about your resentment list? Any surprises? How does it feel to get them out of your head and onto paper?

. . . .

. . . .

What do you stand to gain from doing this work? What's the benefit in continuing with your autism discovery?

. . . .

. . . .

What will you preserve by closing this book (literally and metaphorically!)? How will you benefit from not exploring what autism means for you?

. . . .

. . . .

YOUR AUTISM DISCOVERY DEAL

I want to learn and understand what autism means for me in the following areas of my life:

. . . .

. . . .

. . . .

I hope further awareness and acceptance of autism will create the following changes for me:

. . . .

. . . .

. . . .

I know that this exploration will be uncomfortable for me at times. If I find it overwhelming, I will speak to (name(s) of friend/family):

. . . .

. . . .

. . . .

I'm ready to explore what autism means for me, what it gives me and what I need to take care of myself.

If you feel inclined to make it a self-declaration to note a turning point in time:

Signed: . . . .

Date: . . . . / . . . . / . . . .

I hope that getting your thoughts out and on paper has cleared some space for you for moving forward in your exploration of you and autism.

 If you're struggling to know how to respond to some of the prompts in this book, that's okay. You're here and you're considering some major things about yourself and your life, and that is to be celebrated.

Remember, it's okay to say 'No! Not that,' and explore you and autism in the way that works for you.

If you're further down the line with your exploration, writing down your resentment and fear can still be relevant.

I accepted myself as an autistic woman a couple of years ago and I still feel resentment and fear about being autistic!

My resentment and fears evolve as I do. I've become more active in speaking out about the changes I want to see in education for young autistic and neurodivergent people.

The pushback from those who wish to keep their convenient status quo can stir up a lot. I need to know when to pause and take a break. Writing about the blocks, the feelings that can make me paralyzed, continues to help.

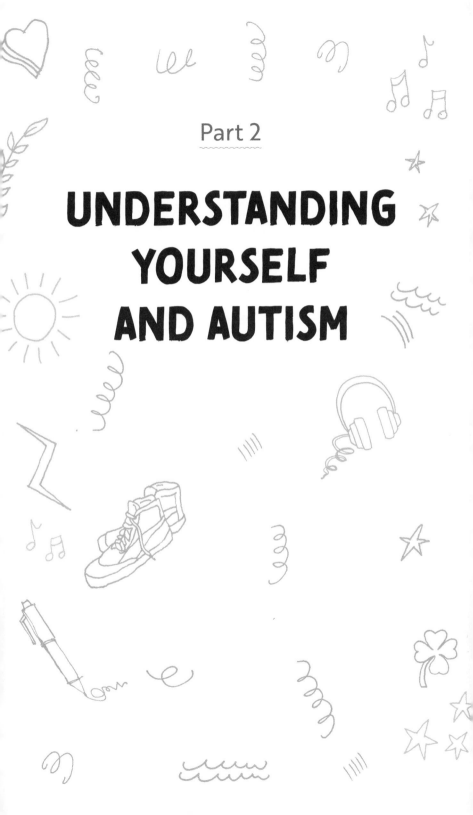

Part 2

UNDERSTANDING YOURSELF AND AUTISM

CHAPTER 3

TRIGGERS FOR LATE AUTISM DISCOVERY

My autism discovery came through it being identified in my child. This will not be a discovery route for everyone.

In this chapter I cover the likely triggers of late-life autism discovery. I hope you find a familiar experience that mirrors whatever triggered your discovery. When we see a familiar experience, it can help us to feel seen, heard and validated.

You may not find a trigger story here that matches your own experience; yours may be a rare route into autism discovery!

Or it may be less dramatic than a trigger; it may be a slow dawning, a slow cumulation of conversations or little signs.

The purpose of considering our autism discovery dawning is to reflect more deeply on the clues that were there along the way and to consider more deeply the significance of the eventual turning point for you.

We will touch on the brain-body connection as a route to discovery. This is an area worth contemplating here, as it's often in our body that clues show up for us that can be linked to other areas of life that are causing crisis for us.

The Tipping Point for Neurodiversity to Be Widely Accepted

One thing I know is there will be a tipping point in all of this. From it being a whisper, a rare topic of conversation, to something that you notice being talked about more on TV, in the media and then all around you in friendship groups. It will be talked about so much more that it's normalized and it will become mainstream.

Until one day, in the not-too-distant future, it will just be.

It won't be rare or controversial, it won't be shameful or unusual; it will be an accepted, understood way to recognize neurological difference. A different way of thinking, experiencing the world and communicating within it.

For that to happen, we need to amplify our voices, our stories, to openly share our experiences, both good and bad. We need to join together to create a tipping point.

A key part of oppression of marginalized groups, the mechanism or root cause of oppression, is making people think they are defective (Rae, quoted by Price 2023a and 2023b) on a very individual level.

This is why we cover different routes into autism discovery here – to illuminate the, often-difficult, experiences people are having that lead them to discovery and to bring late-discovered stories to the surface for a better awareness everywhere.

For those who are bewildered and struggling in life and yet to discover their autism, reading or hearing about a late-life autism discovery experience that they can relate to might just be the thing that leads them to their own discovery.

We need more visibility of autism and how it can present for different people, along with the strengths it gives us and the struggles we can face.

I hope that in the future, women, non-binary people and people of colour will be able to discover their autism earlier in their lives and that this will vastly improve their quality of life. That will happen when young people have a reference point, stories and visibility of people who look like them and are wired differently too.

Burnout

From all the stories I have read and listened to, burnout seems to be by far and away the biggest trigger for late-discovered autists exploring autism.

For many autistic people, the cumulative effect of many years of working in noisy, busy, fast-paced environments, constantly in meetings, expected to meet increasingly stretching demands and targets and dealing with constant changes and uncertainty, will cause high levels of exhaustion.

These environments are hugely stressful for autistic folk; they affect our sensory processing capacity and stretch tolerance levels that will affect our ability to mask our direct communication preferences and ability to navigate the social demands.

Managing these levels of stress daily, weekly, monthly and annually will cumulatively take its toll on us.

If we are not able to get regular rest and recovery time, this stress will lead to burnout.

In talking with Sue Freeman, who I met in one of my autistic communities, about her late-discovery triggers, she shared that ultimately a severe bout of burnout was what led her to discover her autism:

> Looking back, I can now see that in the year or so leading up to my autism self-discovery I was heading for, and then firmly in, severe autistic burnout. During this time, I was dealing with stresses in multiple areas of my life and increasingly I wasn't coping. I didn't have the language to explain what was happening to me. I knew that something was very wrong and I was getting worse and worse.

The burnout may start in small bursts and then may become more prolonged until the many burnouts cause a complete autistic burnout.

Autistic Burnout

The National Autistic Society refers to a study carried out in 2020 (Raymaker 2022):

> Autistic burnout is a state of physical and mental fatigue, heightened stress, and diminished capacity to manage life skills, sensory input, and/or social interactions, which comes from years of being severely overtaxed by the strain of trying to live up to demands that are out of sync with our needs.

Autistic burnout is characterized by pervasive, long-term (typically for three or more months) exhaustion, loss of function and reduced tolerance to stimulus. It causes us to struggle to function in every single aspect of life, much as Sue experienced in her debilitating autistic burnout. It also greatly affects our ability to deal with any kind of stimulus.

Whilst this is not something I've had diagnosed, I have certainly experienced a couple of episodes of autistic burnout in my life. I found the last episode of it really frightening; for the first time in my life, I was really scared I wasn't going to recover from it. I lost all motivation and self-belief and it took almost a year to recover. I had to surrender to just stopping and resting until I was able to cope with the basics.

I have heard some women describe having a breakdown as being the trigger for them to explore underlying causes. Their descriptions of their breakdowns have many similarities to autistic burnout.

Given that the study mentioned above was carried out so recently, many of you who may have had a severe bout of burnout prior to 2020 may have had it assessed as a breakdown.

My hope is that now the definition of autistic burnout is backed up with the findings of the study, this may start filtering through to general health practitioners who can then help people to explore autism for themselves.

For so many late-discovered autists, periods of burnout or breakdown have been misdiagnosed as depression or chronic anxiety disorders, which has led to them being treated with incorrect medication.

Whilst there is no doubt that undiscovered autism and the stress of living in ways that are unnatural to the autistic mind can cause so much stress and anxiety, it also has damaging effects on mental health, which over time can lead to mental health conditions such as depression and acute anxiety. Treating the effects of these conditions will not address the underlying challenges of autism.

How does autistic burnout resonate with you?

. . . .

. . . .

Mental Illness and Misdiagnosis

In all this time of autism being unrecognized in females, I find the most alarming and sinister aspect of it to be the mistreatment of women.

Many women are misdiagnosed as having bipolar disorder when in fact they are having regular meltdowns in response to dysregulation, which is when we can't control or regulate our emotional responses, and overwhelm.

The patriarchy and medical establishment's underlying rhetoric, still today, is that any heightened emotional responses must be tamed, numbed and silenced for the convenience of others.

Interoception, the sense that informs you what is happening inside your body, and alexithymia, the ability to recognize and understand your emotions, can play such a huge part in eating disorders, which can in itself be a huge clue to autism. It hasn't yet been established how common eating disorders are for autistic people. It is recognized that sensory differences related to food, a need for control through familiarity and food counting becoming an intense interest can be reasons for someone developing an eating disorder.

Mental Health Support

I've heard positive examples of people seeking psychotherapy or counselling to help manage their mental health, and this may become the trigger for or a route into learning about autism or neurodivergence.

It's becoming more common for private practice therapists to open up about their own neurodivergence, which can start a helpful conversation and lead to a client exploring this further for themselves.

As more information on autism becomes widely available and therapists are doing their own research, they might be the one that asks that all-important question, 'Have you considered autism as a reason for you finding some aspects of life challenging?'

Right now, in the UK, access to mental health support is dependent on your privilege and resources.

How did your mental health play a part in autism exploration?

. . . .

. . . .

Major Life Events
COVID Pandemic

For many of us, the COVID pandemic in 2020 was a turning point in a variety of unexpected ways, with many people's carefully constructed worlds changing overnight.

With our regular routines and habits stripped away, we were left with gaping holes to deal with.

For some, there was a huge amount of comfort in the overnight change of the stress of our daily lives, full of unexpected changes, sensory challenges and communication hurdles, being removed. It brought us newfound peace.

Suddenly, not only was working from home allowed, it was mandatory. Unless, of course, your role was 'on the front line', a term that became a regular part of our vocabulary.

Busy cities suddenly became a place of peaceful solitude, all traffic silenced.

All of this gave us time to listen deeply, internally and externally. It gave us time for our busy, contemplative minds to notice. To notice deeply our own thoughts and to consider patterns or themes in the challenges we've faced in life.

This is certainly true of my experience of autism discovery, with it coinciding with the beginning of the pandemic, where suddenly I had slow days and time to really explore me and autism. I often wonder if I might have just ignored the signs and put off exploring it more deeply were it not for the experience of living through a pandemic in those early days of my autism discovery.

For many of us, it brought about deeply meaningful conversations with those in our lives.

There was *no small talk*! Not in the beginning of the pandemic anyway – it was all talk on a much more meaningful level.

It wasn't all peace and solitude though, was it?

For those of us with a family under one roof, trying to navigate and negotiate what time was available for us to work and rest, whilst trying to manage parenting, schooling and providing emotional support to our children and ageing parents, it was a *lot*.

For some people, living in a pandemic, with this level of uncertainly and loss of regulation, became the turning point for them.

For James, not being able to cope with living in lockdown, under one roof at all times with his family, and the loss of any kind of routine took its toll. His mental health was so badly affected he had to seek medical help.

It was lucky that his doctor listened carefully to him and referred him to a counselling service called Time to Talk; luckier still, the person James spoke to said to him, after 20 minutes of him sharing his struggles, 'Have you ever considered you might be autistic?'

This should not be a story of luck, but James's turning point and access to the right people is still a rare enough experience that it is considered lucky.

And, given the lack of understanding of how autism presents in women, it is difficult not to wonder if a woman with the same feelings of struggle that James describes would have been listened and responded to in the same way.

Through an autism lens, what impact, both positive and negative, did living through a global pandemic have on you?

. . . .

. . . .

Pregnancy/Birth of a Child

Whilst it wasn't a route to discovery for me, the event of becoming a mother caused more frequent autistic meltdowns, exhaustion and overwhelm that I struggled to manage. When my previous method of treating huge life events like new work projects to be managed didn't serve me in new motherhood, and I lost independence, I found life really difficult to cope with.

I can still see the questioning faces of the participants of a mother and baby music group I took my first baby to when he was ten days old! He slept through the entire thing as I self-consciously shook a maraca and left, conceding that treating motherhood as a work-style project was not going to work!

What major life events caused a crisis for you that you can now see was amplified because of autism?

. . . .

. . . .

Your Child's Diagnosis

The first murmurs of our child's difference came when he was aged three. 'Do you understand him? It's difficult to understand what he's saying,' said the nursery school manager as I was trying to navigate a speedy exit when picking my son up.

Someone was banging a tambourine, music was blaring, hands were being clapped and there was a lot of noise and movement coming from the 50 or so preschool kids in the nursery school setting.

I felt anxious and overwhelmed, at both her question and trying to keep my son nearby. He was prone to running off in the opposite direction from the one I was heading in. I felt his frustration and he had his hands over his ears, something I increasingly noticed him doing.

What followed this moment was the first of the hoops we had to jump through to explain away a beautifully different child, endlessly curious and enthusiastic about the world and most definitely not ticking the 'normal' milestone boxes.

Not initiating play, happy to play alone and merely playing by the side of others, sometimes ignoring the person calling his name. He seemed more upset by changes than other children and was mighty keen on independence and exploring the world in the way he wanted to, not the way he was expected to.

No one directly told me they were assessing him for autism. The speed at which assessments and visits came was alarming. I felt I was being tested by the parent 'police', judged against a measure, a standard of 'normalness' that I knew deep inside I did not meet myself.

I felt terrified of autism at this stage. I was very ignorant of what autism was. All I had gleaned was from snippets of conversations and articles about how a child could suddenly go from being smiley and loving to uncommunicative and unaffectionate. Within the mothering circles that I was on the edges of, there was still the hangover of the discredited theory that autism was caused by childhood inoculations.

It became my unconscious mission to ninja away any detection of autism in my child. I successfully managed to persuade speech therapists, health visitors, paediatric doctors and then teachers, for quite some time, that our son was simply introverted and preferred being in his own imagination than in large groups.

In my own undiscovered neurological difference, I was navigating the world with huge amounts of internal anxiety that made my drive to please people and hide from them consume a lot of my waking energy. It was this drive that misguided me in the belief that the safest thing to do was to cover up any hint of difference – in both me and my children.

It took another five years for autism to finally catch up with us. It took me witnessing the extreme stress and overwhelm my child endured at school – whilst we were at a school social event, now known as the 'quiz night from hell' – for me to finally realize, with a much-needed jolt, that in pushing away or choosing to ignore the differences that existed in my child, I was causing him unintentional harm.

After the 'quiz night from hell', my husband and I sat down with our son to chat about it. 'That was a bit stressful at the quiz last night, it was so noisy! What was it like for you?' I asked.

'It makes my brain hurt. My brain is very tired. It's like trying to download 20,000 voices all at once,' said our son.

As well as being a total joy and a way to communicate his thoughts and ideas with the world, drawing is a sensory soother for my child. When we were having this conversation with him, he drew us a picture of him with his hands over his ears. Lots of speech bubbles with 'Blah blah blahs!' Inside his head, his pink brain is tired and so sad, and it's imagining a faraway quiet land.

'What can we do to help you to find it less stressful?' we asked.

'Will you find someone who can help me understand my brain?' And so we did.

We found an amazing clinical psychologist called Dr Kat who helped him and us to understand autism. She helped us to create tools and a language to understand and help him manage the magnitude of anxiety he was navigating in trying to live in ways that were unnatural to him.

The autism doors were opened for us, and in the increasing amount of reading I was doing about autism, two words kept leaping out and started looping in my mind: 'genetic link'.

Instinctively, I knew I was that genetic link.

Once we'd started this process of understanding autism for our child, it was a short, but very difficult leap for me to start exploring how autism can present in females.

In Chapter 4, I will focus on those initial raw reactions you have when the penny is fully dropped and your consciousness is fully aware of your own autism.

My autism discovery trigger and turning point, the point of no return, can be very firmly fixed to the 'quiz night from hell'!

Looking back, I can feel compassion for myself in how frightened I was about my child standing out, in my actions in trying to help him to fit in. I can also see that in my desire to protect, I was also unintentionally harming.

I was giving the message, 'You have to behave in this way to be seen as normal; it's not safe to be different.'

This has played a huge part in me going on to explore my own difference and to find peace in it. I do not want to impose a message on my beautiful boy that his difference is 'wrong', so I have to untangle myself from that.

If you are doing the same exploration for yourself, or considering it for similar reasons, I send you a whole heap of love.

Brain-Body Connection

The brain-body connection is an area worthy of contemplation here as it's often in our body that clues show up that can be linked to other areas of life that are causing crisis for us.

Chronic Health Conditions

A link has been established between neurodivergence and a number of co-occurring conditions such as Ehlers-Danlos Syndrome (EDS) and joint hypermobility, the common symptoms of which are gastrointestinal issues, increased pain and extreme tiredness.

In an episode of Linda Bluestein's 'Bendy Bodies with Hypermobility' podcast, Dr Jessica Eccles talks about a study she has led to explore the link between joint hypermobility and neurodivergence.

In the study, she found that the neurodivergent participants were four times more likely to be hypermobile than the neuro-typical participants. Furthermore, it found that 60–80 per cent of people who are neurodivergent and hypermobile are female.

Again, in talking with Sue Freeman, a friend who discovered she is autistic in later life, about her autism discovery triggers she shared:

> I was already living with a bunch of chronic health conditions, including hypermobile Ehlers-Danlos Syndrome (hEDS). The only way I'd made sense of my chronic health symptoms a few years previously was to dig into the research before beginning a long journey in seeking professional help and eventual diagnosis. The first diagnosis was of hEDS in 2016 and then diagnoses of other co-occurring conditions followed in subsequent years.
>
> So here I was again, trying to make sense of what was happening to me, and as before, I dived into research. I began to read about the emerging links between hypermobility and

neurodivergence, in particular the research by Dr Emily Casanova in the US and Dr Jessica Eccles at the University of Sussex Medical School, as well as the work of autistic advocates online. Suddenly it all made sense!

So many neurodivergent people could be living healthier lives, without pain or trauma, if this information were widely available, healthcare professionals were adequately trained in autism and neurodivergence, and the brain–body links were researched. If you'd like to find out more about the brain-body link, you could explore the work of Dr Jessica Eccles and the charity SEDSConnective, led by Jane Green MBE.

What brain-body connections, if any, do you now make? How can autism affect you physically (e.g., pain, exhaustion, recurring illness)?

. . . .

. . . .

Sometimes There is No Trigger...
Sometimes Autism Finds *You*

Sometimes we grow up feeling different for our entire life. We don't know why or what it is; it's like a puzzle with a piece missing – we spend our lives looking for the missing piece.

The missing piece somehow finds us when we are ready to see it.

For so many women, it's the click on an article on the internet, it's the TikTok videos where we can recognize something of ourselves in what is being shared about autism or attention deficit hyperactivity disorder (ADHD) that makes it click – that's me!

What was your turning point or the thing that triggered your autism discovery? Write about it here:

. . . .

. . . .

What were the other clues that you now recognize as being part of your autism discovery?

. . . .

. . . .

When you start to delve deeper into the life stories of other late-discovered autists, you might find it heavy or it might bring a great deal of sadness to the surface. Many autists feel things really deeply; we may be strongly emotionally empathetic – we feel the emotions that we sense or imagine others may have felt, especially if being treated badly.

At times I feel like the world is too big and I am too small and insignificant in it. If you have feelings similar to this, which may have surfaced as you've read other triggers to discovery, I urge you to go and do something lovely for yourself that will help to regulate you or make you feel like you are taking good care of yourself.

You may experience overwhelm on a regular basis with the volatility and tumultuous crisis we face. Knowing when to switch off and to find peace amongst it all is really important, especially as an autist.

I cover more of this in Chapter 10 when we look at creating your Autist Care Instructions. Go and look at it now if you want to consider what taking good care of yourself as an autist means for you.

CHAPTER 4

NAVIGATING THOSE EARLY DISCOVERY DAYS

In this chapter we'll explore the first reactions you have when you become aware of autism and how it relates to you and the way you live your life.

The first reaction can be very raw and powerful, and the reverberations from it can last.

To help you reframe the rest of your exploration of what autism means for you, there are a couple of activities in this chapter to shift your perspective and change your internal dialogue.

I will share with you the very first reaction I had when I first read about how autism can present in women. I kept a record of it and every time I read it back I feel more compassion for myself and the weighty fear and shame I was carrying about it.

My first reactions are full of judgement and harshness. I think that it's very relevant to share that with you, because you may feel like that yourself.

We need to make space for an honest dialogue with ourselves; those harsh reactions hold really valuable information and insight about emotions or barriers that lurk beneath.

My initial feelings have changed as I have come to accept myself as autistic. My thinking will continue to develop and evolve the more I engage in the neurodivergent community. Yours will too.

In parts of this chapter I refer to autism living in me. It has been pointed out to me, on more than one occasion, that this can make it feel as if I'm describing autism as if it's an alien!

I have purposely left those references in here because I think this can be part of what happens when we process this very new concept of how we see ourselves.

Autism can feel alien at first; you can look at it with disbelief and instinctively want to reject it, like it doesn't belong to you. That is all a natural part of the process of getting from awareness to acceptance of yourself as autistic.

When I started exploring what autism means to me and who I am, I got very confused about the language around it. Is it 'person with autism' (person-first language – PFL) or 'autistic person' (identity-first language – IFL)?

This can become quite a heated point in the autistic community! The truth is: it's down to personal preference.

I felt that once I'd accepted that autism is a huge part of me and affects everything about me and my identity – how I experience and interact with the world, then I was really accepting myself as an autistic woman – I am autistic.

This might be something to stay curious about for yourself from this chapter through to the end of the book.

The most important thing is that you accept what works for you and what you truly believe in how you relate to your autism.

Once I've shared my insights with you, the remainder of this chapter will be for you to reflect on what resonates and to focus on your first realizations and raw reactions, followed by an activity to remember who *you* are.

This chapter is designed to help you to start delving deeper into the unravelling that happens when you see yourself and your life from a new perspective. The benefit of this is to develop a deeper self-awareness of the resistance and barriers you might have about processing this new information – to consider *yourself* and *autism* on a deeper level.

My Raw Reaction

Here's an email I sent to my husband on 14 February 2020 (romance is not dead!):

Subject: mmmmmmm......... where to next?!

Buckle up, we're in for a bit of a ride with this Autism... Asperger/Aspie thing I suspect... First and foremost it is of course about our wonderful boy.

As I've started reading more and more I can't help wondering about how it might live in me.

I may wave the white flag with getting anything done today, as I'm disappearing down a bit of a rabbit hole with reading about Asperger's and Asperger's in Women.

This article is one I've found most relatable, so I thought I would share with you https://everydayaspergers. com/2012/02/10/aspergers-traits-women-females-girls

Stuff I can relate to:

- Lack of spatial awareness!
- Seeming selfish as I always turn the conversation back to me! (it's because I make sense of the world from the inside out)
- Being shit at domestic stuff!
- Straight talking
- A bit innocent and naive at times
- Noticing exchanged looks, in groups of women and being utterly perplexed about what it means... but knowing I've probably said something strange
- Never quite knowing what people think of me (except with a trusted few) I often walk away from conversations feeling disconcerted, feeling like I've had a strange interaction (I am a strange interaction!)
- Feeling safe at home and why having a safe space is so important to me
- Holding grudges following deep hurt
- Being excellent at hiding and escaping!

- Feeling 'fizzy' after a lot of time around people
- The joy of having space to myself, no longer having to have a 'mask' on

Will you still love me now you know what a weirdo I am?

I'm having a bit of struggle with some of this. It's partly comforting and partly unsettling as it's illuminating my strangeness even more!

That's all for now xx

When I read that back today, I am struck by many things.

I am struck by the fear that I was feeling back then, struck by how hard I am on myself, struck by all that judgement I had of myself – labelling myself weird, strange and unlovable.

I remember sending that email to my husband. I remember that day of getting stuck down a rabbit hole (I am remembering another women who suspected her autism emailing me and using the same phrase when she started reading these articles too!).

Midway through reading all the described traits on Marcelle Ciampi's (aka Samantha Craft) 'Aspergers Traits (Women, Females, Girls)' blog written in February 2012 (mentioned in my email above), a good and lovely friend of mine called.

I did that usual thing I do when my phone rings, look at it in horror and weigh up if I have the energy to speak with the person calling me!

I was mid-sob when Kathryn called, she's such a lovely friend, so full of warmth and love that I pressed the green button.

When your voice is heavy with tears it's a dead giveaway! 'Are you okay? What's wrong?' asked Kathryn.

'I'm reading this blog about women with autism and I just know that it's me!' Strangely, I remember the thing I was most concerned about, as outlined in my email above, was that my husband would no longer love me!

'He won't love me anymore, now he knows what a weirdo I am,' I wailed to Kathryn.

She, quite rightly, replied, 'Well he's a bloody weirdo anyway, so don't worry about that!'

I share this with you, because maybe you feel like that? That you're a weirdo?

If you're an adult starting out on the exploration of autism and yourself, you may have been carrying a sense of your difference all your life, never understanding what it might mean for you but feeling strange because of it.

There will always be a first reaction. It will be strong. You can finally see your truth in black and white. When you know, you know!

Raw Reaction Record

Your first reaction to considering that you may be autistic can be very strong and raw, and it can shape the rest of your discovery journey.

You've spent most of your life, up to the point of discovery, considering yourself to be a certain way. And just like that – reading words that resonate so strongly you know them to be your truth – that self-perception will totally unravel. Once seen it cannot be unseen.

This activity will help you to explore that reaction in more depth. It will give you more information about what's shaping that reaction. This can give you more space to start looking at it from a different perspective.

RAW REACTION RECORD

What was your very first reaction to reading about how autism can present in adults?

. . . .

. . . .

. . . .

What was it in the description that you most related to?

. . . .

. . . .

. . . .

What were the paradoxes in your first feelings and reactions?

. . . .

. . . .

. . . .

What judgements did you have about autism and how you might be viewed as an autistic person?

. . . .

. . . .

. . . .

What feelings do you think are underneath those judgements?

. . . .

. . . .

. . . .

Autism Traits

I cannot write in totality about every single autism trait and how that might be lived and experienced in those who identify as female.

There is a Reading and Resources section at the end of the book where you will find places you can access more information on, amongst other things, extensive autism traits.

Much, much more wide-reaching and extensive research is needed on how autism is experienced and can present in females as both children and adults, as well as people of non-binary gender and people of colour.

The social bias of what's expected of females puts huge pressure on us to cover up any clues that may show we do not reach society's expectations. Research also needs to look into how these traits can be masked, and the findings need to be considered in how autism is assessed in females from children through to adults.

Structurally, I see autism as having key features that affect how we experience and interact with the world:

- Sensory processing
- Communication
- Social interaction
- How we organize information and tasks – executive functioning

We'll each have unique experiences and expressions of those features.

Underneath those features are characteristics or traits – they can define our autistic identity.

This next part is about you starting to identify your autism characteristics or traits. My aim is to help you to understand yourself and autism on a deeper level.

I'll share what I understand to be the key characteristics of my autism to provoke deeper thought on how it plays out for you. Some things I share might resonate or help you identify alternatives in your autism characteristics and traits.

My Lived Autistic Traits and Characteristics

Here's what stands out for me as traits or characteristics to understand my lived experience of autism:

Deep Thinker

I am a very deep thinker. I can consider things on many different levels, including being aware of my own thinking process.

I have recently become aware of a ticker tape-type news flow that flashes through my mind when I am in conversation with more than one person.

What does that frown mean? Am I talking too much? Do they want to leave now – how do I wrap this conversation up? Am I talking too loudly? Am I showing enough interest in what they are saying? Should I be talking to that person over there? She looks really bored – am I boring her? How can I bring this conversation to an end?

I can still pay close attention to the conversation and what is being said. And now I am also aware of the new level of conscious thought that is happening whilst I'm in group conversations.

I'm sure that ticker tape thinking has always been there; but now I understand my autistic mind better, I am conscious of it.

There are times I wish I could switch my brain off! I wish I could have no thoughts at all. Just silence.

The best thing about being a deep thinker is it can offer solace and can be a place to hide; my own imagination is a wonderful place to be. Given my own way, I could easily fritter away and entire day just daydreaming, just thinking!

What, if anything, is resonating with you in exploring the 'deep thinker' trait?

. . . .

. . . .

Highly Sensitive

Being highly sensitive is both friend and foe, a gift and an affliction.

The number-one misconception about autistic folk is that we lack empathy.

I recently learned that there are two types of empathy: emotional empathy and cognitive empathy.

Emotional empathy is where you can empathize so deeply with another person you can feel what they feel.

Cognitive empathy is when you can predict what someone is thinking.

It's the emotional empathy that is one of the big traits of my autism. I feel the emotions of others so deeply. I can tune into the changes in atmosphere in a room. At times this can be overwhelming. Mostly it's useful information now that I can identify that the feeling is external to me.

The upside of being highly sensitive is the feelings of joy and wonderment I can experience from a beautiful day, travel and experiencing a new place with all the sounds, smells, colours, textures and flavours. Nature, and the changing of the seasons, feeling the sun on my face and hearing birdsong around me bring me deep joy.

Absorbing the joy of children or babies, hearing other people laugh, catching a smile from a stranger walking past can lift my spirits, and the image of that connection will stay with me as a visual reference for a while.

Music has a huge effect on me. I am highly sensitive to it, often finding myself in tears or with a huge grin on my face from listening to it.

Growing up, I was always described as sensitive and shy. This was rarely a compliment, nor were these traits seen as valuable. In a world where we are conditioned to think that chattiness, resilience and sociability are keys to success, shy and sensitive are overlooked and undervalued traits that are often followed by, 'She needs to develop more confidence in herself.'

In British culture, highly sensitive and overly emotional are derogatory terms, and I feel a strong need to challenge that thinking!

For me, it's a much-loved trait of my autistic mind. My feelings are how I make sense of the world. Being highly sensitive is my sixth sense; it's my intuition about people. When their words and actions don't match, I can rely on my deep sense or intuition to guide me on whether I can trust them. It is never wrong!

How does emotional empathy play out for you? What does it give you? What difficulty does it cause?

. . . .

. . . .

What resonates or differs for you about being highly sensitive?

. . . .

. . . .

Rhythm of Life

It's often said that autistic folk are rigid and struggle with changes to routine.

I don't like to consider myself rigid – who would?! Due in large part to a lifetime of people pleasing, driven by an anxiety 'fawn' response, I have gone out of my way to make myself adaptable – your flexible friend! This has come at a high cost to me.

It's taken me a while to fully understand and accept that living with uncertainty or constant changes causes me stress and dysregulation.

The build-up of dysregulation affects my anxiety levels. If I have no time to rest and recover from the build-up of dysregulation, it leads to meltdowns, shutdowns and eventual burnout.

Whilst I don't want every moment of every day to be set in stone, I crave patterns: a flow, a rhythm that works.

What causes dysregulation for you?

. . . .

. . . .

What helps you to recognize that you're dysregulated?

. . . .

. . . .

Understanding that I'm autistic has enabled me to be more aware of the things that do cause me stress, to acknowledge that the things out of my control and constant changes in life can be stressful to me and take a lot of energy to adapt to.

One of the key features of my autism is a place for everything and everything in its place. There needs to be a system and a flow of how things can be located, stored and accessed.

This is all well and good if you are the only keeper of that system, but chances are that, like me, you are not the only keeper of your 'dream' systems to keep life flowing with ease!

What affects your rhythm of life?

. . . .

. . . .

What could help you to acknowledge or manage the unsettlement from dysregulation to your rhythm of life?

. . . .

. . . .

Intense Interest

Special Interest in Humans

Autistic folk have an enthusiasm, passion and excitement for things that deeply interest them. These interests can change over time; they might have an overarching theme, but the special interests will vary in topic as we grow and change.

I have, and always will have, a special interest in humans.

The subheading to this is how humans behave, learn and develop. How you can unlock their potential and create environments for them to thrive and grow.

What are your intense interests or passions?

. . . .

. . . .

Do your interests have an overarching theme?

. . . .

. . . .

Chameleon

A big part of my autism has been about experimentation with my identity. At times this has been fun and playful, but mostly it's been about trying to fit. As a child, I would mimic the look I saw in the girls at school or on pop stars. As an adult, I would mimic the look I see in the women thriving at work or in social groups.

From a very early age, I instinctively understood that a large part of acceptance was about how you look.

As a teenager, my bedroom walls were covered in images of female pop stars or female icons I was curious about.

I was interested in how the glamour of their appearance could give these women power; only I wanted to use this for myself to blend in, not to stand out.

I still know the power of changing 'look' or hairstyle and will continue to do this as I age, defiant in my belief that I shall not be tamed by the patriarchy!

> Has experimentation with your 'look' featured in life or quite the opposite?
>
> . . . .
>
> . . . .

Camouflaging

Camouflaging is starting to become recognized as a trait of female autism. It is present in some males and those who identify as non-binary, but mostly it is a trait of female autists.

If the chameleon trait is a playful and experimental way to fit, the camouflaging trait is more of a survival technique.

Like the definition of camouflage, it is a defence or tactic either by design in nature or in the military to blend in with your surroundings or hide or disguise your presence.

The cost of camouflaging is high. It can lead to a loss of sense of self. At its most damaging, it is said that those who camouflage their identity are most at risk of suicide (Cassidy *et al.* 2019).

The UK Autistic research charity Autistica (n.d.) has found that autistic adults who do not have learning difficulties are nine times more likely to die from suicide. Cage and Troxell-Whitman's (2019) research team also reported that camouflaging is a strong predictor of suicide in autism.

Camouflaging became a conscious way of life for me from age eight onwards. It has allowed me to create the illusion that I understand what is going on and that all is well with me, when often it is not.

Camouflaging started to become more amplified in me as a teenager at secondary school.

I tried to make myself invisible so that no one would take

any notice of me at all. This did not work; instead, it made me a target for bullying.

I made a conscious decision to make myself noisy from that point onward. In conjunction with creating a 'look', I became a noisy, extroverted performer, which gave me the camouflage of being confident, witty and fun.

I was able to adapt to different personas and use different scripts for different circumstances and people. I was able to quickly learn the words, music and dance of different social groups, conscious of mirroring the body language of the group and those most popular in it.

Being completely honest with you (why wouldn't I be? I am autistic and this is another trait of autism!), I am not entirely sure when I am camouflaging now or how to stop.

Having a stronger sense of self now – knowing my values, what matters most to me and what I stand for – means that I don't push myself to mimic others.

But I think there are elements of 'performance' in many of my everyday interactions with people that still camouflage my autism.

I do wonder if I will ever be able to stop camouflaging my autism as a natural reflex. It has been a way of life for almost 50 years.

I do notice the camouflaging more, like a subtle accent shift when talking to different friends. And like most changes, self-awareness is always the key to growth.

I hope in time it will become more natural to me to speak my truth and ask when I don't understand than to camouflage.

A more detailed exploration of masking and unmasking your autism is included in Chapter 8. There are activities to help you identify how you may be camouflaging. Head to that chapter if you're curious about how camouflaging plays out for you.

How do your autism traits differ to the ones detailed in this chapter?

. . . .

. . . .

Remember Who *You* Are

This activity is designed to help you look at yourself from a different perspective. As we grow older and more conditioned to be responsible and sensible, wizened from the hard knocks of life's disappointments, we can lose sight of the very essence of ourselves and what brings us joy.

We are often our harshest, most brutal critic in our internal dialogue. This can paralyze us, preventing us from pursing activities aligned with our natural strengths.

When looked at through a lens of the trauma that can be experienced from living a life feeling 'wrong' and rejected by a social construct that doesn't work for the natural autist mind, this really amplifies that harsh internal dialogue and connection to our natural essence.

The next activity is designed to help you reconnect with your very essence.

This is important for you as you continue with your autism discovery. So, wizened inner critics: shhhhh! Please suspend your disbelief for the time it will take to complete this activity, because the information you gather will be of huge benefit to you in reaching acceptance of yourself as autistic.

REMEMBER WHO *YOU* ARE

Find your favourite photo of yourself as a child. Take a note of the following when you are sitting quietly looking at that photo:

1. What do you notice about yourself in this photo?

   . . . .

   . . . .

2. What stands out the most about *you* in this photo?

   . . . .

   . . . .

3. What do you *love* about the person in this photo?

   . . . .

   . . . .

4. What are your *hopes* for the person in this photo?

   . . . .

   . . . .

5. What do you *feel* about the person in this photo?

   . . . .

   . . . .

6. What do you *remember* about the person in this photo? What was life like for them?

   . . . .

   . . . .

7. What are you most *surprised* about when you look at this photo?

. . . .

. . . .

For each point above, circle or highlight the word that stands out most.

Now, with the word you've selected for each point, write:

1. I am . . . .

2. I am . . . .

3. I am . . . .

4. I am . . . .

5. I am . . . .

6. I am . . . .

7. I am . . . .

This chapter is a major step forward for you! You have just explored yourself and autism more deeply.

If you've spent time looking more deeply at that very first raw reaction you had when you considered yourself and autism, I really hope it has helped you to shift your perspective a bit. We all carry an unconscious bias – stuff that we're not aware of and have little control over. It's important to bring it to the surface and consider it, without judgement.

I realized from considering my raw reaction that I had been carrying an internal dialogue that I was a weirdo, strange. I was carrying an unconscious bias that to be in any way different made me strange. I was carrying a lot of ableist views in there too. I focus more on this in Chapter 11.

In this chapter you may have explored your own autism traits as part of considering autism on a deeper level. This is just the start of considering autism on a deeper level.

If you felt ready, I hope you remembered how bloody wonderful you are! So often we have a crushingly unkind dialogue with ourselves, berating ourselves for tiny mishaps or mistakes.

Accepting yourself as autistic is a lot about being more compassionate in how you take care of yourself and your needs. Shifting your internal dialogue to one of kindness is a major part of that.

CHAPTER 5

REPLAYING LIFE THROUGH THE AUTISM LENS

In this chapter we'll explore what comes after the initial shock has worn off – once you've had that raw reaction, what comes next? The replaying of your entire life through the autistic lens is what comes next!

It's not an all-at-once-in-a-major-flash-before-your-eyes-type event (phew!). Over weeks, months and years, you will start to replay some difficult times you had growing up, painful rejections and difficult and bewildering interactions; you'll start to remember them again. Only this time you have new information and that will help you to see those difficult times with new information; it will help you to create a new perspective.

It's important to see this replaying of life through a new lens for what it is: information – data with a difference.

You'll be able to see why those life events, interactions and relationships were challenging. You'll see how autism affected the way you interacted and how you so desperately wanted to just get it 'right' like everyone else you could see doing it so easily, 'fitting' in and seemingly having a lot of fun with it.

In this chapter I will share with you what it was like for me to replay life through the autism lens. I describe much of it as 'The Horrors'.

The thing is, it was 'The Horrors' when I lived it the first time around, when I was so desperately trying to get it right and show the world that I was just like them. When I relooked at some of my most difficult times through the autism lens, it became possible for me to be compassionate to myself – to my past and present self. In particular, I started to feel a lot of love for my younger self, and that brought me a lot of peace.

As difficult as it can be to replay life (for me, this meant remembering the shame and embarrassment I felt for what I saw at the time as the most horrific of mistakes and fuck ups), there comes a point where you start to see your neurodivergence for what it gives you, not what it takes away.

One thing we don't shout about enough, in all this talk of all these people finding out they are autistic later in life, is the utter joy there is in being autistic – the *autistic joy*! Of music that makes you want to burst with glee, of birdsong that sounds orchestral, of laughing at your funny literal thinking and how absurd and silly it can be.

For there is another side of all this exploration of how difficult it was to navigate life and wondering why life stuff – like friendships, exams and fitting into big groups and hierarchies of people – was so difficult and perplexing.

Once you've understood and made peace with your neurodivergence, accepted it and embraced all the bloody brilliant things about your autistic self, you can experience the joy of just enjoying all that you are and all that your wonderful brain brings you in seeing situations, problems and possibilities differently comes.

The essence of this chapter is about helping you make sense of the emotions you are feeling as you progress through your autism discovery. Making sense of this will help you to move forward, to not get stuck in those feelings and to get clarity on what insight they are providing you with.

There are a couple of activities that will help you take your exploration even deeper – exploring 'The Horrors' and the 'happy house' of joy (finding compassion for yourself).

Buckle Up

Once the initial shock of realizing that you 'have autism' wears off, buckle up, because if your experience is anything like mine, replaying your entire life through the autism lens is quite the rollercoaster!

By design, the autistic mind has a good memory for detail. Coupled with strong emotional empathy, recalling painful memories can mean it feels like they are actually happening again in the moment of recollection.

My tendency to internalize and focus inward on challenges being somehow caused by me or things being my fault, rather than looking outward at cause and effect, meant that this is where I spent the early part of replaying life through a new lens.

What has been coming up for you in replaying your life through the autism lens? Brain-dump the threads of what is emerging here:

. . . .

. . . .

What's been the most surprising memory to resurface?

. . . .

. . . .

What are you starting to see differently about those memories now, as you replay them?

. . . .

. . . .

Shame

Having used alcohol as a social lubricant to navigate my way through social interaction with groups, I have spent a large portion of my adult life dealing with 'The Horrors'.

'The Horrors' are when you wake in the morning after a night out and instantly replay the night before. This will involve visual replay of your behaviour, actions, terrible dance moves, etc. Thanks to the alcohol intake, both the act of self-perceived cringey bad behaviour itself and the recollection of the horror will be greatly amplified, meaning it feels a million times worse than it actually was (although perhaps sometimes it really was as bad as you suspect!).

It will also involve the replay of your words, snippets of conversation, your loud laugher or cheeky retorts.

Rarely do you replay the actions, words or movements of the other people involved. Because, obviously, no one else's behaviour was bad or a reason to trigger a 'horror'.

A large part of replaying my life through the autistic lens felt like 'The Horrors'.

In no particular order, here are some of the painful memories of my difference I relived in acute detail.

Being bullied at school. Lending people money that was never paid back and knowing now that there was never any intention to repay it, because when you're autistic, particularly at an early age, you believe pretty much everything that people tell you.

All the (many) times I had been loud, annoying, full of bravado, cheek and swagger that did not match how I felt inside – and being taken down publicly for these things.

All the times I had been overwhelmed with stress at work, leading to public meltdowns. The public panic attacks I had when presenting to people – panic attacks in boardrooms.

The rejection I have experienced from friendship groups, such as returning from holidays and the group I had gone with ghosting me, and (still) being utterly perplexed as to what it was I had done but knowing it was something annoying and shameful.

Being rejected from the heady height of an organization

because, whilst I was very good at my job and got great results, I could not do politics.

Lacking in cognitive empathy, being unable to guess what someone was thinking, being unable to read the cues... when replaying life through the autism lens, I was worst hit by the revelation that it was the one who was nicest to my face who twisted the knife most deeply.

The vivid recollections of the play dates from hell (all of them!) for both my autistic son and me.

'Oh, you're an embarrassed mum!' – the recollection of one of my mum friends illuminating my utter shame as I was unable to get my youngest son to stop misbehaving, whilst trying to keep hold of my overstimulated eldest son who was running away from us with his hands on his ears.

The list of 'The Horrors' goes on and on and on.

The shame of getting it wrong. The shame of not fitting, the shame of not understanding why. The shame of the loneliness, of having no one to turn to who could help me understand, of the isolation this caused.

The shame for the inability to stand up for myself. The shame of feeling shame of *everything*!

Embarrassment

How does embarrassment differ from shame? Does embarrassment trigger shame or is it the other way round?

I experience embarrassment as an almost physical pain.

The combination of strength of memory coupled with it often looping over and over on repeat in its replay can make it feel like it's actually happening in the moment.

I think that 'Embarrassed Human' pretty much sums up how I have felt throughout my life.

The desire to avoid the feeling of embarrassment in my effort to get it right, to fit in, to not stand out, has required huge amounts of energy.

And I am delighted to tell you that this is one of the best

things about getting to acceptance of being autistic: I don't feel embarrassed anymore.

Write a list of the feelings and emotions that are surfacing for you as you progress through your autism discovery.

If you struggle to understand your emotions, draw what you imagine is happening for you as you replay life with new information.

. . . .

. . . .

What information are those feelings giving you?

. . . .

. . . .

Comfort

Alongside all the shame and embarrassment I felt when replaying my life through an autistic lens, I also felt comfort.

This replaying of life does not follow a straight line.

Once the floodgates are open, prepare yourself for all sorts of memories that you had pushed down into a dark hole reappearing.

I found a great deal of comfort in information about autism. Not all of it resonated, and some of it is utter nonsense.

When it does resonate, or helps you explain why some aspects of life have been such a challenge, it is such a comfort.

Ah, that's why. I understand.

It makes sense! I make sense!

For all the isolation and loneliness I felt, I also suddenly felt a deep sense of belonging that I had never really experienced before.

I finally felt that I was not alone. At least on paper.

I was also able to start to consider the strengths that my autism gives me.

My autistic strengths have allowed me to create a business I love; it's called Who I Am!

Working out *Who I Am* – and understanding my identity and direction – has been a lifelong exploration for me! I now help others to connect with who they truly are and to work out the path that will bring them the most joy in natural expression of themselves.

Love

At times, when I was replaying my life through a new lens, I felt a lot of love for myself, especially the younger me.

Wow! You navigated all of this, the weight of shame and embarrassment, feeling lost and unsure of yourself and life. You navigated it all on your own.

You never gave up on learning. Learning how to improve, how to grow.

You never gave up on doing this so that you could help others to unlock their potential to create environments for them to thrive!

I have always been interested in working with teenagers, young women in particular. I want to help them get clear on what matters most to them, their values and their value in the world. To help them to understand their strengths and for them to define success on their own terms.

Replaying my life through this new autism lens really helped me to see that so much of that desire stemmed from having such little sense of who I was, particularly during my teenage and early adulthood years.

At times, this led to me being in danger.

Mostly it just heaped on me a lot of unnecessary shame, embarrassment and lack of self-confidence or sense of self.

What comfort are you finding in understanding yourself and your life through the autism lens?

. . . .

. . . .

What If???

At times in my replaying of my life through the autism lens I felt anger. Why did I not know this sooner?

It could have saved me from so much pain and angst. Some really horrible things that happened might not have happened – I could have avoided them, surely?

What if? What if I had have known these things about myself at a much earlier age. Would I have made completely different life choices? Of course I would!

Dump all your 'what ifs' – let them all out, no matter how petty they might seem:

. . . .

. . . .

Quickly, the anger dissipated. Because, 'what ifs' from the past will only tie you in knots. We are powerless to go back and change the past.

When you replay your life though an autistic lens, you may feel a range of emotions and they may differ to mine.

All of your emotions are valid. All of your emotions are information about whatever challenges you faced and may continue to face.

I hope you find comfort amongst it all too. Comfort that you are part of a *huge* collective of wonderful people, who see, feel and experience the world in a different way.

Together, we can help each other to make sense of what we have experienced.

Together, we can make the next generation's experience of being different a whole lot better than ours!

Replaying your life through an autism lens started when you first read those words on a page or saw something on TV or social media that struck such a chord it stopped you still in your tracks and suspended time for a while.

Replaying your life through an autism lens will continue, quite possibly for the rest of your life. Because we don't remember in one big hit. Present-day events trigger memories, and as you replay those memories afresh with the autism lens, you'll see something different each time.

Well done for looking at the pain and the joy, for replaying it with new and important information.

Take a break when you need it. Go for a walk, put your favourite film on, play your favourite song as loud as you want to!

I know from my own experience how hard and exhausting it can be to be down an autism rabbit hole! That's part of autism – hyperfixating on things that we're interested in!

You might not recognize the signs – hyperfixating can affect interoception. It's time to be compassionate and take breaks when you need to.

House of Pain and the Happy House

Now you've considered what comes up for you in replaying your life through the autism lens, what can you get from exploring this further?

Ultimately, as you move from autism awareness to acceptance, you will start to make peace with those raw and difficult reactions.

The following activities are designed to help you start that process – the process of finding peace amongst the 'horrors' from here onwards.

We'll look at the highs and lows of replaying life through the autism lens through two 'houses'.

In the House of Pain, we'll be actively considering: why? What is that emotion underneath that feeling of horror? This will help you to gain an awareness and understanding of how much these difficult emotions played out and shaped you as you were growing up.

These activities will help you to get distance. As vivid as these memories can feel as you relive them now, that event is in the past and it's time to let those horrors peacefully rest in the past.

In the Happy House, we'll also give space to your autistic joy. Distance can help you to see the funny side or to appreciate how your differently wired brain can see the world in unusual and funny ways.

We will make space for that here. Doing this activity will give you a place to connect with memories of joy – we'll spark autistic joy through replaying life through the autism lens.

That spark will create space for you to bring more of that autistic joy into your life today.

HOUSE OF PAIN: THE HORRORS

Your memories of 'The Horrors':

. . . .

. . . .

. . . .

. . . .

What is it that makes these memories so painful?

. . . .

. . . .

. . . .

. . . .

Write about the *biggest* horror of all:

. . . .

. . . .

. . . .

. . . .

What makes it different now that you see it through the autism lens?

. . . .

. . . .

. . . .

. . . .

HAPPY HOUSE: THE JOY

Memories that make you smile:

. . . .

. . . .

. . . .

. . . .

What joy do you remember? Turn up the dial on the colour, sound, movement – anything in your senses that made it such a joy. What made it so joyous for you?

. . . .

. . . .

. . . .

. . . .

Write about the *biggest* joy of all:

. . . .

. . . .

. . . .

. . . .

How does replaying your life through the autism lens now bring relief?

. . . .

. . . .

. . . .

. . . .

A Letter to Your Younger Self

It is time to give yourself some love and compassion – you made it through this bewildering and exhausting life without knowing quite a large and vital piece of information about yourself!

Write a letter to your younger self once you've considered the following questions:

- What age are you? Which year are you sending this letter to?
- What do you want your younger self to know? What is going on at the time that you are writing about?
- What comfort and wisdom can you offer from your wiser older self?
- What about your younger self are you proud of?
- What do you want your younger self to know about the future? What knowledge might have helped you through those tough times?
- What are your hopes for your younger self?

CHAPTER 6

AUTISM DIAGNOSIS

Would you rather go to a library or a party? That is a question, I kid you not, in the autism diagnosis criteria, AQ50 (Autism Spectrum Quotient, Baron-Cohen *et al.* 2001).

My first thought when I was completing it was, 'Of course I'd rather go to a party! Unless it's going to be a shit party, then I'd rather go to a library!!!'

This chapter is about autism diagnosis. It explores the pros and cons and the practical and emotional considerations you will need to weigh up in considering if you want to pursue a diagnosis.

To emphasize from the start: self-diagnosis is valid and you need no one's validation to confirm what you already know – your lived experience of neurological difference.

The reflections and activities in this chapter are designed for you to get clarity on what is best for *you*.

What do you need to give and what will you get from a diagnosis? Will you get from it what you really need? What are you really in pursuit of?

In all honesty, I found the diagnosis an unexpectedly difficult process. I found the writing of this chapter difficult too! I reread through the diagnosis questionnaires and my final diagnosis report to remind myself of the process and what each part covered. Ouch! It still hurts.

And so, this is another chapter that I start with a whole lot of love.

For many of you, diagnosis may be the validation you are looking for and a form of acceptance that will allow you to start unmasking in ways that make you feel calmer and happier in how you interact with others.

If you do find considering an autism diagnosis and the process of the autism diagnosis assessment difficult, a large part of this may be the person or method of conducting your autism assessment. There are a lot of neuro-inclusive assessments that can be very healing processes in themselves.

Some of you, like me, may find it a really difficult process that brings up a lot of things that either you weren't aware of or take you right back to the most difficult times in life.

One part of the diagnosis in particular really floored me. It's the ADI-R (Autism Diagnostic Interview, Revised, Lord, Rutter and Le Couteur 1994) This is an assessment that gathers information about how you developed as a child. It illuminated information about myself that I still reel from when I read it now, almost three years after it was first gathered.

I don't recognize the child it is portraying. The behaviour described does not match my intentions and I can see how I was so easily misunderstood. The weight of the judgement in the statements helps me to see why I began to mask my obvious difference from a very young age.

It's clear my behaviour was not considered acceptable, especially for a girl, 'You didn't want to share your things with others. This was a problem.'

A girl who won't share?! A selfish female?! 'Off with her head!'

Within some of the relationship dynamics in my life, my behaviour is still seen as unacceptable now. I am finding my way with how best to navigate this. Maybe sometimes we need to compassionately remind ourselves that it's okay that we have to keep a 'mask' on for surviving some uncompromising dynamics (along with setting up some safety parameters for ourselves in doing this).

Much of this process is about seeking out places where we do belong as our true selves. The places where it is safe to show our whole selves without condition or expectation. Those people and those places provide a safety parameter for us.

Autism Diagnosis

You've discovered your autism; you are aware of it. There is no doubt in your mind that you are autistic. Everything you have read resonates with you and your life challenges suddenly make sense.

So, why do you need to get your autism officially assessed and diagnosed?

> If you're considering an autism diagnosis, what are you hoping to get from it?
>
> . . . .
>
> . . . .

This is something only *you* can decide. Is it right for you? Can you navigate the many barriers and hurdles there are to getting an official diagnosis?

From my experience, I share here the benefits and barriers to assessment and diagnosis and the flaws in how autism is understood and assessed in women.

The Benefits to Getting an Autism Diagnosis

Many in the autistic community argue that as most of the autism assessment is about you providing examples of your autism, there is little benefit in jumping though the many hoops required to get a diagnosis.

In part this is true! However, as you go through the rigorous process of completing questionnaires, assessments and gathering *a lot* of information, you will learn more about autism and the challenges it presents to you.

Whilst it might not feel like it at the time because the assessment is a gathering of deficits – the whole medical model is designed to look at what is 'wrong' – in gathering a lot of information about yourself and how you developed as a child, you will also start to see your many, many strengths.

For me, my main driver in getting an official autism diagnosis was validation.

Whilst I absolutely knew with unwavering certainty when I read about the autism traits in women, 'That is me! This is how I live and this is what I cover up,' as time went on, I doubted myself.

How could I not?! I had spent my entire 45 years masking and camouflaging myself to fit. The whole headline of my life was, 'She *doubts* herself!'

Along with the way that a mind will play tricks on you, at times I absolutely thought, 'I have imagined this whole thing. There's nothing "wrong" with me.'

Again, having programmed myself to be like everyone else, to fit, to blend, and being a notorious overthinker, a worrier (a trait of autism: deep thinker), it was quite easy for me to tell myself, 'You're way overthinking this!'

So, validation was, for me, the only real benefit to going through a diagnosis process.

How could I even join in with the conversations about autism without getting officially diagnosed as such?

The truth is: you do not need to validate yourself for *anyone*! Of course you can join in with the conversations about autism; your lived experience of it is what you bring to the party.

And if you're not autistic and want to join in the conversations, do. With curiosity, questions and a whole lot of listening!

The Barriers to Autism Diagnosis

- The only major research carried out on how autism presents has been conducted on white boys. This creates a very biased understanding in how autism is experienced. Within the medical profession, there is generally a very limited and narrow understanding about how autism can present.

- For females, those identifying as non-binary and people of colour, this can lead to doctors not seriously considering an autism assessment or diagnosis for you.
- Given the lack of knowledge and understanding within the general medical profession, if you are in autistic burnout or describing the everyday anxiety and stress you experience from being autistic, it can lead to you being misdiagnosed and then given incorrect treatment/medication for depression, bipolar disorder or acute anxiety.
- For UK-based readers, the NHS wait times for autism assessment can run into several years – the longest I have heard of is a seven-year wait.
- There is *no* definitive assessment for diagnosis in adults. Not one recognized standard that clearly diagnoses autism in adults.

Your Pros and Cons for getting an Autism Diagnosis

Pros	Cons

Emotional Considerations in Autism Diagnosis
How I Found the Assessment and Diagnosis Process

Whilst I entered into the process knowing it was about helping me to accept my autism, I was ill prepared for how disturbing I found it.

In all honesty, I thought the worst of it was over. I thought that the replaying of my life through the autism lens was the really painful bit.

The language used in all of the assessments is about finding flaws, problems, defects. That is hugely unsettling and disturbing.

Every single questionnaire you have to complete feels loaded with judgement, and I wanted to argue the meaning or comparison with pretty much all of them!

The use of words such as symptoms and mental disorder heavily suggests that there is something wrong with you, seriously wrong.

When you've struggled your whole life to 'fit', this whole process weighs heavily and doesn't leave a good feeling.

No wonder some autistic folk might feel inclined to live life on the fringes, keeping invisible for safety... And, with the standards of 'normal' or acceptable defined by pathological deficiencies, no wonder those of us who externally display our autistic traits – questioning systemic flaws and calling out evident hypocrisy, expressing our challenges or discomfort from sensory overload – are labelled as difficult!

The whole medical model, along with every societal institution and system, is currently designed to tell us we are wrong.

It's really hard to have these discussions with your immediate family, too. This formed a large part of the assessment process I went through – looking back at your childhood development.

My mum was incredibly helpful and supportive in providing me with the information I needed. I'm sure she had her own challenging emotions around answering a lot of the deficit-based questions.

Our chosen approach to gathering data for the ADI-R questionnaire was for me to send over the extensive 35 questions about my childhood development. I sent them to her in three parts, as it was too much for both of us to digest this in one go!

After she'd considered the questions, I then 'interviewed' her on the phone. I had to write down her responses.

It is not easy to have to write down things like, 'I laugh inappropriately in social situations or too loudly,' and 'I seemed to lack empathy when other people were ill and I didn't realize they were ill unless they told me.'

This one was a killer, '...knew from a young age there was something very different about me'.

Difficult for her to say to her 46-year-old daughter. Difficult for the 46-year-old daughter to hear, write down and then type up!

'In Summary, My Findings Are You Are Autistic!... How Do You Feel about That?'

It's another level of the kaleidoscope – the mixture of emotions that come when you are officially told what you already know in your mind, body and soul, 'You are autistic!'

I have really come to learn that I find my feelings almost impossible to describe in the moment. I need time to process things; there is often a delay between the event and then the reaction. This leads to all sorts of confusion about what I am reacting to! It's never the minor thing – 'the straw that broke the camel's back'.

I have also learned that much of my love for romcoms and family dramas is that they allow me to feel all the emotion that's often linked to how I feel about events in my actual life!

When my clinical psychologist shared her findings with me and asked me, 'How do you feel about this?', my answer came completely from a place of logic. This is how I should be feeling; 'I feel happy!' I said, whilst feeling not at all that way inside!

'I feel happy because it backs up what I suspect.'

But I didn't get the feelings of joy or validation that I was seeking.

It was too raw. I was shaken up like a snow globe. It would take some time for that to settle.

Support Available Following an Autism Diagnosis

As neurodivergence becomes highlighted more in the media, both in the traditional reporting of journalism and in self-reporting in social media, new services and support are emerging, and I hope that this continues to evolve as our knowledge and community grows.

There is no support available following an autism diagnosis through the NHS for adults in the UK.

Once children are recognized as autistic via the NHS, some support is provided through the education system. This support is inconsistent across the UK and, without exception, desperately underfunded in every region of the UK.

Often support is in the form of an intervention. How can we make this child comply with our models of behaviour that is deemed 'normal'. This is not the support that is needed by any neurodivergent child; it leads to shame, stress, trauma and mental health challenges.

I think my views are made pretty apparent throughout this book! Systemic change is needed everywhere! This is something I focus on more at the end of this book when I explore the positive changes we need to put in place for neurodivergent folk to thrive.

The headline of these views is 'change the environment not the person'.

If you have the resources available to fund private support, there are many wonderful neuro-affirming therapy services becoming available that focus on healing the trauma you may have experienced through a lifetime of not understanding and covering up your own neurological difference.

Neurodivergent assessments that look at many neurodivergent traits in one go are also becoming available. For example, the often co-occurring autism and ADHD are included in one assessment.

Co-occurrence of neurodivergent traits is a common factor in many neurodivergent humans. The recognition of this and a more holistic way to assess and understand these neurodivergent traits as part of one assessment rather than multiple difficult individual assessments is the way this needs to develop, and fast.

The neurodivergent lid has well and truly been lifted, and I can't wait to see what develops and unfolds for us in this community of alternatively wired human beings!

Your Pathway to Discovery

This activity is designed to give you an overview of the best way for you to approach an autism diagnosis.

Self-diagnosis is valid, and if that's the best route for you, stick with it.

For too long you've followed the rules set by others, and discovering something so huge about yourself later in life can be the turning point that sets you free from playing by the rules of a game you did not want to join in with!

The benefit of exploring what you will get from an autism diagnosis and what you will need to give in order to get it is clarity.

Getting clear on what matters most to you and what is right for you will give you an outline of a plan for your next steps.

Give: What will I need to give to get an autism diagnosis?	Get: What will I get from doing this?
If NHS is the route I have to pursue, how long am I prepared to wait?	What really matters to me most about an autism diagnosis?
How much time can I set aside to complete assessments and fill out forms?	
How much time can I dedicate to meeting with my chosen clinical psychologist?	
Is there a good time in the year for me to dedicate to this?	
If I can pursue a private assessment, what is the total amount I can invest in this?	What am I really looking for in pursuing an autism diagnosis?
What's the emotional investment required for this? What will be the cost to me emotionally?	
Am I ready to look back at my life's challenges through a medical model?	
If I go private, what is important about the psychologist I choose to work with?	Can this need be met in other ways?

Looking back at this 'Give: Get' overview, is self-diagnosis my chosen route?

I really understand how difficult it is to even get to the point where you are considering going further into autism awareness towards acceptance that you are autistic.

Taking this further to get a diagnosis or deciding self-diagnosis is right for you is a big choice and a big step forward in you claiming a new part of your identity.

You might approach it and then back away from it, over and over. That is okay too. It's taken this long to discover autism may be part of you because the information was not available to you.

There is no time pressure or limit on taking this next step.

I see it and hear it when I talk with those who are curious about being autistic or newly discovered autists. They get tangled up in knots of doubt – 'I think I am autistic – it makes so much sense – but how can I be?!'

'I think I'm just overly anxious and thinking about this too much.'

'The more I think about it the less sense it makes. I just want it to go away now!'

'Maybe I am just bad at life!'

As I tell them, gently and with a whole lot of love, it is your deep inquisitiveness and search for the truth that's the biggest clue to your autism. Deep thinking and endless questioning – that's a major autistic trait.

It is deeply uncomfortable to leave behind the security of seeing and understanding yourself to be a certain way, especially when deeply coded within you, from the earliest of ages, was a longing to fit – to be just like everyone else.

I acknowledge your courage to follow your curiosity and quite possibly a lifelong tumultuous search for your own truth. I celebrate that you are here, reading these words, contemplating these questions and taking the time to deepen your own self-awareness – it's the basis for all of us to grow.

Once you start to trust your own truth, to stop running yourself ragged with questions and sit with, 'Okay, I am autistic, so what?!'... you might be surprised. It's not as bad as you might think!

Let's take some time now to acknowledge and celebrate yourself for working through this level of your autism exploration.

I am acknowledging myself for:

. . . .

. . . .

I'm celebrating that:

. . . .

. . . .

CHAPTER 7

TALKING ABOUT AUTISM

It takes a lot of courage to share something new and deeply personal about yourself. This is what you'll be doing when you choose to share your autism discovery with other people.

This chapter shares some of my insights about the reactions, the myths and lies you may hear in response to sharing your autism with others.

I am sharing this because I want it to help you either prepare for some potentially perplexing reactions you may receive or make sense of responses that can feel hurtful.

We'll look at what might be behind some of these reactions and responses to help see them from a different perspective.

We'll also look to illuminate the knowledge gaps that still exist and the work that needs to be done for autism to be widely accepted. This work is not for you to do alone; do not be burdened by constantly having to educate people about autism, especially if you are just starting out with developing your own understanding of it.

Once I've shared my insights and experiences it will be over to you to start looking at what this means for you.

There will be questions in the form of journal prompts to help you to explore who you want to share with, what you want them to know and how they can help you beyond this point.

There is an activity that will help you to keep a record of the different reactions you receive as you share your autism and how your feelings to these reactions evolve over time as you get more comfortable with the self-acceptance of your autism.

As I was becoming aware of my autism, replaying my life through the autism lens and grappling with any kind of acceptance of it, I gently started to share it with people.

The first two people I shared it with, outside of my immediate family, gave me the most encouraging and loving responses; I will be eternally grateful to them.

Interestingly, I shared my awareness of my autism with them in text messages as I find written communication easier than spoken communication.

As I started to get more and more certain of my autism, I started to speak it aloud to the people I spent time with.

For sure, I will have communicated it with the uncertainty and shame I was feeling about my difference. I know the first few times I spoke it aloud, I immediately doubted myself and felt deep shame at having uttered the words.

Often after I had spoken it aloud, I would immediately say to myself, 'What the hell are you sharing this for? You are completely imagining that you're autistic, you don't even know for sure that you are.'

I did know for sure. You will know about your autism, for sure. As soon as you read about it and resonate with the traits, characteristics and challenges. As soon as you do your first online test for autism. You will know for sure.

And we're autistic, and therefore we overthink things. Be patient with yourself. Getting from awareness to acceptance is not a straight line. You will overthink it! You will be influenced by what you read. You will read a lot... you're autistic!

Who do/did you most want to share your discovery of your autism with (most trusted family and friends)?

. . . .

. . . .

What help and support do you want from them as you continue to explore your autism?

. . . .

. . . .

What do you want them to know about your awareness of your autism?

. . . .

. . . .

Reactions

The array of reactions you get when you share your discovery of autism will be surprising and probably not what you want to hear.

Here are the themes of the reactions I experienced when I shared my awareness of my autism.

'Everyone's a Bit on the Spectrum'

This is the most common and the most frustrating reaction you are likely to get from people.

It invalidates the importance of your discovery and the weight of its meaning for you.

It may differ in its tone. There could be a well-meant intention behind, 'Everyone's a bit on the spectrum.' For example, 'Don't worry, we are all different in our own way, there's nothing to ashamed of.'

It could also be used as a response to the tone in which you are sharing your autism discovery. I know in those early days of uttering it aloud to friends, my tone was one of shame, defence and self-disgust. I was wracked with concern about what lay ahead of me in the unfolding of my difference.

When you're feeling this way, you're likely to hear, 'There's nothing special about you, everyone's got something different about them, get over yourself!'

In the spirit of the definition of neurodiversity, coined by Australian sociologist Judy Singer to create a political movement of recognition and inclusion of the neuro-minorities, we are *all* neurodiverse... there are no two brains alike!

So, let's bust the myth and prepare you for the most common response you're likely to hear after sharing your autism: 'Well, everyone is a bit on the spectrum, aren't they.' No, not everyone is on the autistic spectrum. As it stands now, it is estimated that 1–2 per cent of the population are autistic. With improved research on how autism presents in female and non-binary folk, and therefore more accurate identification and diagnosis of autism, I think the percentage of the population who are autistic will be much higher. But not everyone will be a bit on the autistic spectrum – you either are or you are not.

If the person who says this to you can relate to autistic or neurodivergent traits or characteristics, they are likely to be autistic or neurodivergent themselves.

'Are You Sure You're Autistic?!'

This reaction can be difficult to receive because its inference is one of doubt that what you are saying is true.

The reaction infers that you cannot be correct in your belief or that there's something wrong in being autistic.

'Are you sure you're autistic?!' can also be about the person's perception of you. We all have perceptions of people – of who we believe them to be based on our experiences of and interactions with them. Our perceptions can also be based on how we feel about a person and how they make us feel.

In their mind, you do not strike them as what they perceive to be autistic.

Each and every one of us will have a perception of what autism is. Chances are, you do not line up with the perception of autism, especially if you are a woman, non-binary or a person of colour, because most of the research is biased on white boys.

And herein lies the problem. Most people are misinformed about what autism is. This will be based on what they read in the media, what they see on TV and how they see autism portrayed on-screen.

So forgive the person who reacts with disbelief to you sharing your discovery of autism. It is highly likely their understanding of autism and how it presents in women and minority groups is poorly informed.

It could be that their understanding is based on poorly informed portrayals of autism only existing in women who are geniuses, amazing at maths or blunt to the point of rudeness with an inability to make friends or interact with humans.

Whilst our perception and understanding of autism is improving, on the whole, it is still by far and away inaccurate.

The more we late-discovered adults, autistic women and people from marginalized groups feel safe to speak up and speak out to challenge the stereotypes and incorrect beliefs, and the more we share our lived experiences of being autistic, the better informed people will be.

'You Don't Seem/Look Autistic!'

This seems utterly ridiculous! What exactly does an autistic person look like?!

Whilst it's not directly questioning your belief that you are autistic, the person who is making this statement believes the same myths and lies that we saw in the previous section.

They have a fixed view in their mind of what autism is and how it presents, and that view doesn't fit with how they experience you.

Take a deep breath when you get this response. As you get closer to acceptance of being autistic, it does get easier to be curious and interested in what others have to say about autism.

A big part of getting autism widely accepted and creating environments for neurodivergent folk to thrive is creating a culture where it is okay to ask, not to tell or guess. For difference to be accepted, we need to get curious.

'Autism Is So On-Trend Right Now!'

Oh how I would love to respond to this utterly ludicrous statement with, 'Yes, my brain is *this* season's colour!' Or '*Yes*! Autism is the *shape* of the season!'

Autism is not a trend! It is wonderful that more and more late-discovered autists are sharing their stories of their experience of being autistic. We need awareness of autism before we can get to acceptance.

'Autism Is Completely Over Diagnosed!'

Brace yourselves, neurotypical world! The more we understand and demand access to information and support for our environments to be adapted to suit neurodivergence, the more this will become the new style... it's here to stay, darling!

Neurodivergence and autism are going mainstream!

'Congratulations!'

This is the most wonderful reaction of all to you sharing your discovery of your autism.

In the spirit of checking in on each other, staying in touch and being more open about how we were feeling during 2020, I had a wonderful, intimate exchange with a mum friend on a WhatsApp message.

I then felt safe to share with her my newly discovered autism and that of my son. 'Congratulations! That must be really exciting for you both.'

It was such a joy to receive this response. She is absolutely right; it is really exciting to discover something that helps you to make sense of yourself and your world.

It's wonderful to know your truth, to understand your difference and why some things can be such a challenge for you.

It's such a relief to discover a language for your difference and to know there are other people who are different, with similarities to you. It is deeply comforting to make sense of you and the world around you with this new information.

'I Have an Autistic Friend. Would You Find It Helpful to Chat to Them?'

This is such a positive response to receive from a friend. You feel seen and heard. To know that you can access other women's lived experiences is so helpful.

I did take up this offer of talking to a wonderful autistic woman, who fully embraced her autism and had all the wisdom of what comes next – after discovery.

Diagnosis? She was able to talk me through the whole thing. What she'd found helpful and what she hadn't.

It took me weeks to pluck up the courage to get in touch with her! And it felt like a big step forward too.

The autistic woman I spoke to, Rachel, was all sorts of wonderful. Straight-talking, swore like a sailor (I love a *big* swear!). We shared some similarities and, of course, a lot of differences.

We both have autistic sons and that had played a big part in our own realizations. Rachel had done a lot of work with autistic children and had really helped her son's school to put some things in place that made it a great learning environment for him.

I have a kind of super recognition of people, particularly in voices. I regularly freak out the people who work in my opticians when I ring up. I recognize their voices and remember their names, which makes them a bit unsettled (especially as I only ring them twice a year!).

I recognize people's faces easily. I may not have even met them before; I might have seen their social media post or seen them chatting with someone else I may or may not know. I make connections in a network easily, understanding how people link together by putting together their connections.

It's actually quite hard not to blurt this out if I get introduced to them. Often I just do say, 'Oh, you know so and so,' or 'You used to work here,' or 'I saw you at this event,' quickly followed by, 'I'm not stalking you! I have a freakishly good memory for people!'

Rachel has the opposite. She can't remember people's faces: 'face blindness' (prosopagnosia). She often has people chatting to her about previous conversations and thinks, 'Oh my God, I don't even remember meeting you!'

I found talking with another autistic woman when I was newly discovering my own autism helped me to make sense of what I was processing.

It also helped me to see that where I was with my feelings was temporary. I could see that I too would get to acceptance for myself.

And it helped me to understand how I would benefit from getting a formal diagnosis, which is definitely the next layer to the onion of it all! Unravelling life through a new lens and then getting input and gathering more data was an important next part for me.

How helpful would it be to talk to other late-discovered autists or another autistic woman who has accepted their autism?

....

....

What would you like to know from other late-discovered autists or autistic women?

....

....

'How Do You Feel? Has It Cast Doubt or Helped to Understand Another Level of Your Personality? What Has Changed for You, if Anything?'

This was another wonderful response I received from my insightful and curious friend Amy.

Sit with her wonderful question for yourself for a while. What comes up for you?

Take Good Care of Yourself: Some Things to Consider Around Sharing Your Autism Discovery

'Share the Scar not the Wound'

When you're still processing your newly discovered autism: choose very carefully who you share it with in the beginning, as you are still getting your head around it.

The first few times I spoke to trusted friends, it was barely a whisper when it came out. There was uncertainty and disbelief as I said, 'I think I'm autistic.' Sometimes I wondered if I had imagined that I was autistic.

I know I had strong feelings that if I didn't have an official diagnosis, I was completely wrong.

It was very raw and shocking back in those early days of reliving my life through a new autistic lens.

I was carrying disbelief, doubt, embarrassment and guilt, which was wrongly making me feel judged.

Proceed With Caution: Things to Consider Before You Share Your Autism Discovery

> Sometimes people's reactions are surprising, and they may reflect their lack of awareness and understanding about autism.

Their reactions may also be in response to any strong feelings of doubt or uncertainty you are displaying when you share your newly discovered autism.

Certainly, the 'We're all a bit on the spectrum' comment can be driven by a need to make you feel safe and 'normal', to reassure you that you belong or that the person you are sharing it with wants you to know you are loved, no matter what.

Respond, don't react! Stay curious and interested in reactions.

If you can, listen to the reactions or responses with curiosity. Consider: what's behind what the person is saying? What might be influencing their response? What does their reaction say about their lack of understanding about autism?

This gets easier the closer you get to acceptance of being autistic. The rawness has gone, the need to defend autism and yourself has lessened and you become unapologetic about it.

When you get to acceptance, you are more equipped to give information or respond rather than react.

Oversharing is an autism trait. If this trait applies to you, it's okay if your autism discovery spills out. If you're finding it hard to process and are judging yourself for it, you may receive reactions in this way; you may feel judged by others.

Autism is genetic. There may be family member(s) who are unknowingly autistic. Once you know the traits of autism and how they can present differently, you're likely to suspect other family members are autistic.

It's not up to you to tell people they are autistic!

You can only do the work for yourself; from awareness to acceptance. You can *never* do it for someone else, no matter how obvious it might be that they are autistic! (I know this from painful experience.)

When to Share Your Autism Discovery

If you're still processing, especially if you're replaying your life through the autism lens and reliving pain, you are not ready to share your autism publicly.

Do the work for *you* first. Have a small group of trusted people who you might reflect with or share where you're at.

Before you share more widely, get to internal acceptance for yourself.

When you feel like you have fully reached acceptance that you are autistic and proud of it, then you're ready to share it with the world.

Sharing and Safety

Many people might not feel safe to share their autism discovery within their family unit or wider community – more is covered on this in Chapter 11 where we explore ableism.

A big consideration for you in sharing your discovery more widely is psychological safety. Psychological safety means there's a shared belief that it's okay to speak openly, to be vulnerable without consequence – permission to be candid without negative impact.

There is still much work to be done across society in creating psychological safety for people to show up as their true selves. Many businesses have cottoned on to the value of the neurodivergent brain. 'Share your neurodivergence with us!' they might tell you – especially if it's Autism Acceptance Month or Neurodiversity Celebration Week.

Often they haven't done the groundwork of training staff to understand what neurodivergence is and how it can present. It's unlikely they have done the work to really explore the unconscious bias that exists within their organization.

The reality to this is it might be psychologically safe for a white cis male to share he's autistic but not so much for anyone else to share they are autistic/ADHD (AuDHD) or dyslexic.

It is a privilege to share your autism or neurodivergence. Not everyone has that privilege. For some in communities that are marginalized by race or class, it is not safe for them to share their neurodivergent discoveries within their own communities, let alone with the wider world.

I greatly admire the work of Praveen Kolluguri, who describes himself as a neurodivergent troublemaker! And Atif Choudhury, CEO and co-founder of Diversity and Ability. They write and speak powerfully about the work we need to do to get to intersectional inclusion. You can find out more about them in the Reading and Resources section at the end of this book. I also mention more about Atif's work in Chapter 11.

A cultural shift needs to happen for people to understand autism and neurodivergence and to explore their own unconscious bias within it.

For too long there has been such a lot of shame about being different, 'other', 'less' and 'wrong'. When we internalize and carry this around individually, we isolate ourselves.

In our isolation, we shrink and believe we are wrong and mistaken in showing our traits, in speaking honestly, in challenging flawed systems and ludicrous injustices, in finding joy in small things, in being excited about our passions and in missing invisible signals and cues.

Collectively, when we feel psychologically safe, we can share our lived stories of our autistic lives – the strengths and struggles and the needs we have – and come together to make it better for others – better for neurodivergent folk to thrive.

For the Record

As you progress in your acceptance of autism, your reactions to sharing your autism will evolve and become responses.

Your very first realization about your autism might have felt raw in the beginning, and receiving reactions when you first start to share might feel that way too.

Your reactions to other people's responses to your autism will feel less painful as you get closer to your own acceptance of it.

The following record can become a marker for you to see how much you're growing into your autism self-acceptance. Record the reactions you receive to your autism over time and reflect on it over the coming months and years.

FOR THE RECORD

Who	When	Their reaction	How that made me feel (my reaction	What might have influenced their response	What I'm left curious about	Next time...

CHAPTER 8

MASKING AND UNMASKING

In writing the chapter about what triggered my late-life autism discovery, and knowing how I feel today – being at full acceptance of being autistic and feeling more liberated than I have ever been – I am struck by how imprisoned I was in trying to guard my son and ultimately myself from autism.

I can tell you that, for him, understanding that he is autistic, learning what challenges that presents and having tools to navigate them has allowed him to thrive, develop a confidence in himself and have the space in his body and mind to engage in activities he would have been too anxious to contemplate before.

So, how was I imprisoning myself in guarding us from opening up to the possibility of being different – to the possibility of being autistic?

In this chapter we'll explore the tool that many of us late-discovered autists adopt from a very young age as a safety mechanism: masking. Masking is the ultimate way to guard ourselves from unwanted criticism, rejection and exclusion.

Masking comes at a very high cost to us. It takes up a huge amount of energy and can rob us of a strong sense of self.

Masking is a complex and complicated safety mechanism. 'Unmasking' is not easy or simple; I still struggle with it today.

 And so I start this chapter with a whole heap of love and compassion. For you.

I want you to know that simply stopping masking your

difficulties, simply ceasing compensating or camouflaging your true self and your needs is not an easy thing.

I have come to learn that 'unmasking' is a privilege that is afforded mainly to those within the 'dominant' culture – white, cis, middle class. I acknowledge it is not without its complications and difficulty for those within those cultures – I know this from my own lived experience. There is much pain and healing that needs to happen for late-discovered autists.

For those in marginalized communities, who have been marginalized by those who keep them oppressed with messages of their deficiencies, inadequacies or wrongness, it is often unsafe to even share their neurodivergent discovery, let alone contemplate 'unmasking'.

For some autistic and neurodivergent folk, it is impossible to mask, or they may be able to mask for some of the time until they are in great struggle and overwhelm. When that happens, they are often rejected or excluded for being badly behaved or difficult.

This is a chapter that you might need to dip in and out of. You may need to take time to keep reflecting on what is coming up and to revisit it when you're further down the line in your acceptance of your autism.

As my autism discovery coincided with a global pandemic, I entered the post-pandemic world as a newly discovered autist, which meant I was weighed down with a lot of anxiety!

I questioned myself a lot about my anxiety during this time. Was it because I felt weird to be socializing again after the pandemic? Was it because I had a heightened awareness of my autism traits? Was it that the world was so much noisier? Or was I just aware of every single sound around me?!

I had also recently learned about my own Rejection Sensitivity Dysphoria (RSD), which is extreme emotional sensitivity and pain triggered by the perception that you've been rejected or criticized by important people in your life. This brought additional challenges around this time, such as constantly replaying conversations whilst newly socializing and searching for clues of wrongdoing or causing unintentional offence or hurt.

The aim of this chapter is to provide you with information about what masking is and for you to consider how this plays out for you. I encourage you to spend as much time as you need on this part – reflecting, noticing and sitting with your observations.

There are thought-provoking questions and some activities to help develop your awareness of masking. There are also some things you might want to experiment with around unmasking. Only do this when you feel ready to and, most importantly, when you feel it's psychologically safe for you to do so.

Be patient with yourself. Spend time considering the people who can support you with this or who you feel safe talking about it with.

Chapter 10 focuses on you developing your Autist Care Instructions – considering the things you need to put in place to take good care of yourself. It's worth considering these things as you experiment with unmasking.

My Masking History

I know not when I decided I had to do all that I could to fit, to blend, to not stand out. I suspect it became deeply ingrained in me around the age of eight.

When I was eight, I moved from my place of birth, Scotland, down south to live in England.

'You talk funny!' I was told over and over. My no doubt beautiful Scottish accent made me stand out in ways that made me deeply uncomfortable.

So I changed that. For a while, I had an English accent at school and a Scottish accent at home, trying my best to fit in with both environments.

It felt like this dual accent business went on for years. I now understand it was only a matter of weeks!

I was busted by my mum when she overheard me conversing in an English accent. 'Why are you talking like that?! Just be yourself!'

The trouble is, when you have learned that how you naturally engage, communicate and experience the world is different to everyone else, you think you need to behave like everyone else to survive the challenges it brings. You lose sight of who you are.

You lose your sense of self when you mask your identity. When you mask your bewilderment and confusion and push all the worry, anxiety and dread to a place inside, you have little sense of who you are.

You become governed and controlled by a fear that is inexplicable. You just know that blending, hiding and pretending to be like the others is the safest way for you.

You also have to make choices about the lesser of two evils! Who am I going to pledge my allegiance to – my family or these much-needed friends??

Sorry, family, I guess you will stick by me, and I can put up with your tutting because there is safety in this home. In this bedroom I can go and escape to, there is no tutting.

In this place of school, I must do all I can to survive.

Just imagine altering the way you speak just weeks after moving house. Imagine learning and tuning into the new phrases, sayings, what people wear and the music they like at the age of eight! And adapting to it all so quickly. I must have been exhausted.

I have always had a 'special interest' in fashion. Clothes, music, TV – I genuinely still love all of these things. And I can see that these things would have given me a lot of information about how to 'fit', to blend in and to find my tribe.

As a tween and teen, finding your tribe is everything. Once you identify the music you like, then you can dress accordingly. The clothes give a signal to the world: this is me and this is what I like, what I stand for.

TV, as well as being an escape, is a form of education. The dialect used, how people interact, how they connect with each other. Especially when it comes to romance – the close-up of the chemistry, the flirting.

Because I seriously struggled with this in real life! Always taking everything literally, at face value and believing what everyone said, especially at an early age, made teenage interactions impossible to navigate.

Experiencing ridicule, bullying and unwanted attention from the opposite sex all fuelled the need to mask and guard.

I was really enslaved to 'fitting' from this point onwards. Until I learned of my autism.

In sharing how I responded to realizing that my son is different in Chapter 3, I felt a deep sense of shame. In my efforts to deflect autism away from him, I was causing unintentional harm.

I shared it with you because I wonder if this is true for you too. Are you causing unintentional harm by deflecting autism away from you?

I can be kind to myself now. I know that I deflected being different because I was so fearful of not fitting, of getting it wrong, that this lifelong 'guarding' felt like safety.

I was protecting myself and I thought at the time that I was protecting my son too. It felt instinctive and natural and like the right thing to do.

It wasn't, and it had the opposite effect on us both.

I feel deep gratitude and admiration for my son for teaching me about autism.

I feel deep gratitude that I don't have to guard the truth or be imprisoned anymore.

When we guard ourselves, when we present a controlled or perfected version of ourselves to the world, we are in fact imprisoning ourselves. Imprisoning ourselves in lives lived for others, not ourselves. Prevented ourselves from authentically accepting who we truly are.

We are tricking ourselves that acceptance comes from external sources. It doesn't. True acceptance comes from within.

The guard is a prisoner too. Is it time to stop guarding yourself?

The following reflection prompts are designed to get you to consider more widely how you are guarding yourself from being authentically you – this might mean guarding yourself from accepting you're autistic.

What resonates with you about this chapter?

. . . .

. . . .

What differs for you?

. . . .

. . . .

What are you guarding yourself from?

. . . .

. . . .

What is the prison you have created?

. . . .

. . . .

Draw it for yourself below:

- What does the prison look like?
- What does the prison feel like?
- What's the light like?
- The smells, textures, sounds?

We all have an internal critic who tells us it's not safe to be vulnerable or to show our differences to the world. What does the guard look like? Draw it for yourself below.

· What are the standout features?
· What's the guard's motto?

What will it take to break out of this prison?

. . . .

. . . .

Who or what will provide 'shelter' (love, kindness, nourishment, encouragement, support) for you when you get out of this self-imposed prison?

. . . .

. . . .

What is on the outside of the prison? What could life be like when you are no longer guarded or imprisoned?

. . . .

. . . .

Just considering how you might be guarding yourself from showing any kind of difference or exploring the concept that there is an internal barrier to letting your 'guard' down is quite a big thing.

I hope that it's starting to open up some choices for you about how you might want to change how much of the autist you is imprisoned – even from yourself!

It is really important for you to know that whatever action you take is your choice. Do not be driven by 'should'! 'I should do this…' is weighty in the burden of doing what you think you ought to, often to please others.

I know there will be a lot of additional barriers that some of you may need to contemplate, and that is not to be minimized. It may not be safe for you to talk about your neurodivergence within your family or community.

If you feel stuck and trapped by the ways that you are having to guard who you really are, please know that you get to choose how you might like to change that.

Masking

Masking is a huge part of being a late-discovered autist. Whether we've done this consciously or unconsciously, most of us will have developed natural reflexes to cope with hiding our unknown difference.

In psychological speak, masking has two distinct categories:

- Camouflaging – hiding, obscuring, blending in
- Compensation – ways to overcome challenges and maintain appearance of independence and success

The following activities are designed to help you raise your awareness about how you might be masking your difference.

Developing a deeper understanding of how you are masking will give you information about yourself. This information will help you make choices about some changes you might want to make to unmask your autism.

Masking all of the time can be exhausting. It requires a lot of your energy to keep anticipating how you need to 'perform'. It can also diminish a sense of self-identity and worth. This is why we're exploring it here as part of your autism discovery.

 Here are some key points I would like you to keep in mind:

- Go gently on yourself. You have developed these camou-flaging and compensating ways to protect yourself from the perceived harm there is in being different.
- Sometimes you do need to mask to protect yourself; it can be a trauma response to any anxiety you feel in certain scenarios. That is okay.
- Take your time. Spend as much time as you need noticing and observing how, where and with whom you mask.
- As part of this exploration, consider who you feel safest with. In Chapter 12 we will explore who accepts you for being autistic and who doesn't and won't. It can be really valuable to consider this alongside your awareness of masking.
- Only start experimenting when *you* are ready to. It might be that you want to be further down the line with your autism acceptance. Some of you might choose to get an autism diagnosis if you think it will help to give you vali-dation and autism self-acceptance. Chapter 6 focuses on autism diagnosis.
- You might practise small actions or activities as you move through the process of getting to self-acceptance of your autism. Or you might just record your thoughts here and revisit them and take action once you've got to self-acceptance.
- You get to choose what feels right for *you*. Doing what feels right for you and not for others, and not to fit with others, is a big part of unmasking.

MASKING INVENTORY

Spend some time reviewing the masking inventory list below. Tick the masking behaviours that resonate with you. Add additional ones that you are aware of that apply to you.

Camouflaging	✓	Compensation	✓
Friendly chatter with *everyone*		Taking on ambitious projects to keep demonstrating what a high achiever you are – even when you're at breaking point	
Saying *yes* to *all* social invitations		Having a collection of social scripts for different people and different groups to keep the conversation going	
Staying at social events when you want to leave		Trying to find excuses for not taking part in social activities – feeling unwell, children unwell, changed plans	
Feeling obliged to organize social gatherings		Asking lots of questions to get the spotlight onto others – trying to focus as much of the conversation on others as possible	
Not knowing or observing your own limits – continuing to work harder to achieve for others even when exhausted or ill		Saying you're feeling physically ill to justify a day on the sofa or in bed when you desperately need to rest and recover	
Not having any boundaries – being available to help meet the needs of others at all times		Drinking alcohol or taking substances to get you through unbearably loud and stressful social events	
Appearing laid back and easy-going when inside your levels of anxiety are through the roof		'Rehearsing' how conversations will go, spending large amounts of time preparing for new interactions, meetings and social engagements	
Being unable to disagree or express your alternative opinions with others		Putting the needs of others before yourself so that you don't appear to be selfish	

Feeling that if you do something wrong or show anything other than happiness and positivity you will be rejected from groups or friendships	Self-effacing, brushing off hurt, embarrassment, bewilderment and shame	
Being unable to ask for reassurance when you can't read what others think of you	Not allowing yourself to be fully thrilled, delighted and excited about possibilities for yourself – better not get ideas above your station!	
Spending huge amounts of time worrying you've done something wrong and are about to lose friends or credibility because of it	Appearing strong, resilient and capable of dealing with any challenge thrown at you, even when energy is running on fumes	
Worrying after every social event that you were too loud and too much or too quiet and too boring	Lifelong plight for perfectionism to deflect your difference	
Having a lifetime of people pleasing and subservience to others, seeking safety in the background	Spending a long time preparing and editing emails/messages to ensure the correct tone and social niceties are included	
Laughing along with jokes you don't understand or find offensive or not expressing displeasure at humour that's at the expense of others	Using humour as a way to deflect – often laughing at your own struggles to invalidate how troublesome it can be for you	
Keeping up with news, popular culture and fashion to be able to contribute and keep your social scripts relevant		
Always smiling, warm and attentive, even when dealing with high levels of stress/ anxiety		
Adapting your voice, 'look' and tastes to suit the group/ occasion (mimicking)		

Choose three items from each of the camouflaging and compensation lists that are your most prevalent or resonant masking behaviours:

· ·

· ·

Add one more item that isn't listed but is relevant to you for each list:

· ·

· ·

Write about painful or difficult times when you can remember using these masking techniques:

Camouflaging masking trait	Compensation masking trait

What are you noticing about any patterns in how you use these masking traits or scenarios where you use them?

· ·

· ·

What is the cost to you of these masking traits?

. . . .

. . . .

Raising Your Masking Awareness
Over the next week or month, note down times you notice yourself masking.

· Is any new information surfacing?
· What do you notice happens to you when you're in masking flow?
· What happens to your body?
· What happens to your energy?
· What happens to your mind?

. . . .

. . . .

. . . .

. . . .

. . . .

Unmasking Experiments
Choices and Changes

Now you've increased your awareness of how you're masking, it's time to consider what choices you want to make. Because *you* get to choose; no one else.

What would you like to change, stop or do differently?

Be Gentle with Yourself

Try experimenting with people you feel safe with. It could be:

- asking questions when you're not sure about how a friend is experiencing you
- saying no to invitations you don't have the energy for
- in a group you belong to, asking a person you trust within the group questions when you're not sure about what's happening
- considering your limits – what is the cost to you of the work, social event or family gathering?
- considering what you want to say *yes* to and what you want to say *no* to.

UNMASKING EXPERIMENTS

Three things I want to try out:

1. ....

2. ....

3. ....

Who can offer you support with this?

....

....

....

....

....

....

....

....

Reflections on My Unmasking Experiments
What worked?

....

....

What didn't work?

....

....

What do you want to acknowledge yourself for?

....

....

What are you celebrating?

....

....

What else do you want to try?

....

....

Part 3

ACCEPTING YOU'RE AUTISTIC

CHAPTER 9

EMBRACING YOUR STRENGTHS AND NEEDS: DIFFERENT NOT DIFFICULT

Curiosity and a desire to understand how things work and how we can make improvements to make things more efficient and flow better are strengths and traits found in many an autistic person.

In a world where compliance is the dominant force in institutions, organizations and society, questions are rarely welcome. Especially when your questions illuminate the absurdity of certain actions, the waste and the undoubted failure that will happen if we pursue the ridiculous!

Many of us late-discovered autists have grown up being told we are wrong to question. That our questions are annoying or disrespectful – how dare we question authority?!

We learn it is easier to be small, quiet and compliant. We abandon our natural strengths; we do not value the things that we're naturally good at! We see our strengths as trouble and actively hide them.

A big part of autistic self-acceptance is understanding our strengths, our struggles and what matters most to us.

Reclaiming our natural strengths, embracing them and allowing them to be expressed freely in environments that are aligned with our values – the things that matter most to us – is part of the healing that happens when you no longer hide who you are

131

and accept that the things that come naturally are not wrong or bad – they are what make us feel most alive!

This chapter is about identifying and embracing your strengths. It's also about recognizing how autism contributes to your strengths and acknowledging your struggles and the challenges you face.

We'll explore what a spiky profile is and all the 'difficult' labels you've been given throughout your life that have contributed to you devaluing your own strengths.

We'll also explore what your values are and what this tells you about environments you could choose to be in that would enable you to be fully in alignment with those values.

The benefit of embracing your strengths and compassionately understanding your needs is that it changes your internal dialogue to one of kindness. It enables you to self-advocate and ask for support and help.

What's Environment Got to Do with It?

Many of us late-discovered autists have grown up thinking we have little choice in where and how we are educated and work.

We've grown up in world that required us first to be loyal 'subjects' and then good 'consumers' (Alexander 2020).

The demand for compliance is the underpinning of capitalism. Do your duty and be a good consumer. Sure, you have choice in getting the 'best' deal for your consumption, but you won't reach happiness or be a perfect human unless you comply and unquestioningly consume.

We have grown up being told we are wrong to question. That our questions are annoying or disrespectful – how dare we question authority!

If we fail to comply, we are difficult – there is something wrong with us. This is key to marginalizing people –making them believe they are defective.

Often it isn't the authority we question but the outcome, for we want to get the most efficient and effective result.

We are different, not difficult.

Our curiosity has been quashed, our confidence destroyed. We are reprimanded for asking questions – seeking more information in our direct fashion. We are not doing it to crush egos; we are doing it to understand and to get the best results.

But fragile egos do get crushed and the keepers of the fragile egos retaliate through ridicule or by making it their personal mission to create misery and humiliation for us at every turn.

Curiosity and a drive to improve things – to make them better, to align systems to create an easy flow... pah! 'You're oversimplifying it!' we're told.

We have strengths of seeing patterns, making connections, asking questions and wanting to make things work better for the good of the customers – the people who use the service or buy the product – our team and the organization. These strengths can be seen as being difficult in controlling environments, where authority and hierarchy dominate.

For my friend, Sally, this is exactly what happened. Her questions and straight-talking singled her out as trouble. There is no doubt that, alongside her neurodivergence, her being female and daring to question the male hierarchy meant she was subjected to heavy punishment and eventual exclusion from the organization where she had previously been recognized as a high achiever and a career she had invested 20 years in building.

Sally has now found a working environment that is much more aligned with her passions and values, where questions and alternative ways of thinking to drive innovation and getting results are welcomed.

It's recognized by Sally:

I can be myself more than before, I feel less pressure and I'm not forcing eye contact anymore. I've noticed the importance of feeling safe to be my authentic self and also experiencing other people who are authentic. When people are not authentic it triggers me.

Genuinely authentic cultures work for autistic people, but there can be no room for half measures, it either is or it isn't authentic. I've experienced being part of a business where many individuals want to drive change for a more inclusive culture but fear being able to openly share their ideas without punishment.

Only in organizations with leaders who genuinely want to welcome difference in and are prepared to create psychological safety for people to talk truthfully can you genuinely work towards an authentic inclusive culture.

For all our challenges in being able to anticipate what a person is thinking or read the social cues, we can certainly feel when something isn't right or doesn't feel right, and we know when it is inauthentic.

Emotional empathy is high for many autists and can be a form of information that can guide us well – when we learn to trust it.

Feeling psychologically safe in an environment is so important not only in being our authentic selves, where we do not need to mask to survive, but also in embracing and using our strengths to their full potential.

'Difficult' Labels

When we do not have psychological safety in our environments and our strengths are not appreciated, with our struggles and challenges being seen as overinflated or self-indulgent, it sends us a message that our difference is difficult.

For most of my life I have carried an internal dialogue that has said, 'What's wrong with me? Why can't I just do X/Y/Z like everyone else can?'

We can carry the labels that are given to us that are code for 'You're difficult and had better change your ways to make it easier for me.'

My recurring 'difficult' labels have been: selfish, overdramatic, too sensitive, lazy, annoying.

What 'difficult' labels have you been given?

. . . .

. . . .

What negative internal dialogue has that created for you?

. . . .

. . . .

What impact have those labels had on you?

. . . .

. . . .

Social Bias Lens

In Chapter 11, we'll explore the ableism and intersectionality that can create bias and unconscious bias. These biases will also affect the expectations of compliance that are placed upon us.

There is a clear gender socialization bias placed upon us that silently dictates that we, females, behave 'well' – that we do not rock the boat or cause problems and make it easy for everyone else around us.

This bias also dictates that we are especially compliant; we are female and must be cooperative, must follow rules and must not question authority.

Be quiet: be soft, gentle and neat, take up little space and conveniently mould yourself to fit our expectations. This quietness includes not showing anger and no strong demonstration of emotion, for we all know that any shift outside of this will label us 'unhinged', 'out of control' or even 'hysterical'.

This bias is amplified for all people of colour – both men and women. For if you dare to assert your concerns, to illuminate bad treatment or injustice or to ask for help for you or your family, wrongly and unfairly, the judgement is that you are 'aggressive'.

Which of those 'difficult' labels that have been given to you, in addition to neurodivergence, are because of race, age, gender or sexuality bias?

. . . .

. . . .

Acknowledging Your Struggles

If you've been labelled difficult because of your neurodivergent strengths, then woe betide you for daring to have neurodivergent struggles and needs!

Of course you have struggles! Everyone does. We all have unique strengths and challenges.

If you've received the message that your strengths are not welcome, then your struggles have most certainly been unwelcome or judged harshly. This leads us to mask both our strengths and our needs.

Overcompensating or camouflaging our needs can be all the more dangerous because, as well as not being able to ask for the help we need, to rest and recover from our challenges and struggles, we go against our needs and work extra hard, with already depleted energy, to ramp up the cover-up job even more.

Take a moment here to get all of those challenges and struggles out on paper.

The things I struggle with most are:

. . . .

. . . .

These are the things that can most affect my struggles (stressors, energy levels, etc.):

. . . .

. . . .

I find the following things present the biggest challenges to me:

. . . .

. . . .

Of those challenges and struggles, the following are affected by being autistic:

. . . .

. . . .

This tells me that my autistic needs are:

. . . .

. . . .

Spiky Profiles

A common feature amongst all neurodivergent folk is the disparity we have between our strengths and weaknesses. The things we're good at we're brilliant at! Things we find hard are really, really difficult for us.

This in itself must lead us to question our strengths – I can't be really brilliant at this thing if I find this other seemingly simple thing so impossible!

The disparity can be created by our challenges with executive functioning – planning, organizing, retaining information, following instructions, becoming dysregulated by constant changes, interruptions or ambiguity, and social interaction such as small talk or making a phone call.

These everyday tasks and expectations, which for the neurotypical person are straightforward and simple, are far from straightforward for those of us who are neurodivergent and they can take up a lot of energy and cause us a lot of anxiety.

Understanding this and accepting yourself as autistic and neurodivergent allows you to fully embrace your strengths and to be compassionate to your struggles and needs.

The following three activities are designed for you to get really clear on your unique strengths and struggles – to get a really good overview of the highs and lows of your spiky profile. We will also bring what matters most to you to the surface – your values.

What will you get from doing one, two or all three of these activities? Clarity on what will help you to feel most alive – embracing your strengths and understanding environments that will help you to thrive and compassionately manage your needs, including asking for help and support from others.

These things will help you to change your internal dialogue and understand the value you bring to the world. They will help you to accept yourself, your autism and what this could mean for how you choose to live, work and play.

It's time to be unapologetically *you*!

YOUR STRENGTHS ASSEMBLY

It's time to acknowledge and celebrate what you're naturally brilliant at.

In the space below, write down all the things that pop into your head that you consider to be strengths or the things that come most easily to you.

My strengths are:

. . . .

. . . .

. . . .

. . . .

From the list of strengths you've written down, circle the ones you consider to be the result of being autistic.

This next part encourages you to ask those you trust and respect the most to share with you what they see as your strengths. As autists we often can't tell what others think of us. It will be helpful for you to understand how those people whose opinions count the most perceive and value your strengths.

Name five people who you value and trust and whose opinion counts to you (friends, family, colleagues):

1. . . . .

2. . . . .

3. . . . .

4. . . . .

5. . . . .

Ask some or all of those five people to write down or email you three of your greatest strengths.

Write down all the words you receive to describe your strengths:

. . . .

. . . .

. . . .

. . . .

. . . .

. . . .

. . . .

. . . .

. . . .

Circle or highlight the strengths that strike you as both true and in line with what you most enjoy.

Which of these strengths come most easily to you?

. . . .

. . . .

. . . .

. . . .

. . . .

Which of these strengths are aligned with your autistic traits?

. . . .

. . . .

. . . .

. . . .

YOUR SPIKY PROFILE

From the strengths you've assembled and the list of struggles you wrote down earlier on in this chapter, take some time to plot your strengths and struggles. Plot them according to how they show up or are experienced. (It's not an exact science! Go with what feels right.):

Ease

Strengths

Difficulty

Struggles

What are you struck by when you look at your spiky profile? Is there a disparity?

. . . .

. . . .

Could any of your strengths help you with your struggles?

. . . .

. . . .

Who or what could offer the most support with your struggles?

. . . .

. . . .

Your Values

Your values are the things that matter most to you in life.

When you honour your values and when you're in environments that are aligned with your values, it makes you feel fulfilled. It feels natural and authentic to behave in ways that are aligned with what matters most to you.

In contrast, when you are unclear on or ignore your own values, when they get trampled on by others or you are in environments that are misaligned with your values, it can cause you to be deeply unhappy.

You may feel undervalued. It can create cognitive dissonance – a mental conflict that occurs when your beliefs and actions don't line up.

I think the other issue for autists, who place a strong importance on truth, is that when you ignore your values it feels inauthentic, like you are living a lie. Your behaviour and outputs don't feel right and neither does the misaligned environment you are in.

This activity will require headspace and time to do it justice. Why bother?! Getting clear on your values can help you consider all the aspects of your life that you could find more joy in – the places and activities that can energize you and make you feel most alive.

When we can bring those things into our life, it has a massively positive impact on our health and wellbeing.

As an autist, it will also give you your biggest insight into the environments that you will thrive in. Being surrounded by like-minded people who share your values is likely to provide you with the psychological safety to be your true autistic self.

BRINGING YOUR VALUES TO THE SURFACE

Think about the *best* experience you've ever had in your life
– go with the *first* thing that pops into your head.

. . . .

. . . .

1. Now, on a *big* piece of paper, write about that experi-
    ence – in all its glorious technicolour.
    –   What was going on around you?
    –   Who was there?
    –   What happened?
    –   What did this experience feel like?
    –   What was it that made it the *best* experience?
    Read the story of this best experience through. Is there
    anything else you remember about it that you would
    like to add? What really stands out about this best
    experience?

    . . . .

    . . . .

    . . . .

2. From what you've written about your *best* experience,
    circle or highlight three to five words that most resonate
    with you. You really love the sound and the feeling of
    these words; they could be anything from what you've
    written – a colour or a feeling. It does not need to make
    sense to anyone else – these are *your* values!

    . . . .

    . . . .

    . . . .

3. This is where the data mining really comes into play – you need to follow your enthusiasm and choose what most resonates and makes you feel most alive.

   For each of the words you have written down above (the three to five words that you most love from your *best* experience), consider what is important to you about the meaning of that word. For example:

   > In my best experience I felt:
   > Free... the importance of that is independence/ choice/ peace/ autonomy/simplicity/liberation.
   > Creative... the importance of that is variety/ possibilities/surprise/flow/instinct.
   > Learning... the importance of that is growth/ opportunity/expansion/challenge.

   . . . .

   . . . .

   . . . .

   . . . .

4. Now you've delved deeper and looked at what's important to you about the meaning of each word, it's time to make a call on your definitive list of values.

   From the descriptions above about the importance of the words you selected, circle or highlight three to five final words that you love and that describe what matters most to you.

5. My values are:

1. . . . .

2. . . . .

3. . . . .

4. . . . .

5. . . . .

Now that you have brought your values to the surface, the next part is consciously thinking, 'Is this activity, decision, environment in alignment with my values?'

It also helps when you have a very strong reaction to something or feel something deeply – did someone or something trample on a value, the thing that matters most to you?

What actions could you take in the next month that will make your values come alive? It can be work, rest or play.

. . . .

. . . .

. . . .

What environments are most aligned with your values? Again, consider work, rest and play.

. . . .

. . . .

. . . .

How are your values aligned with the autistic joy you get from immersing yourself in an autistic passion?

. . . .

. . . .

. . . .

If you've read through this chapter, contemplated and considered the reflection questions or completed any of the activities, you have been focusing on shifting your perspective – opening up a new way of considering autism and yourself.

That very first raw reaction when you consider that you may 'have' autism can be one of strong rejection. 'I don't want to be different!'

You may see autism and your association with it as a huge problem.

I hope working that through some or all of this chapter has helped you to see, in a positive light, that you are different not difficult!

If you've asked people who matter to you to share how they perceive you and what they consider you to be great at, I salute you! That's *huge*! You might have had to battle some mighty strong RSD to even ask for and then receive their perspective of you.

It takes courage to open yourself up to people to ask them to help you get a greater understanding of yourself.

You might have had a hard time really absorbing the strength they shared with you, dismissed it or thought they were just being kind. Go back and look at those words again – that is what you bring to people, to the world.

It's time to accept all the brilliant things about yourself – let yourself receive the love that they want to give you.

Yes, you'll circle back and question it – that's what we autists do! Let the data you've gathered from others be your constant reminder of what you bring to the world.

Whether you involved others or not in gathering your strengths, considering those strengths through an autism lens can help you to enjoy what autism brings.

For there is such a thing as autistic joy! When the senses you seek out are most alive or you're knee-deep in one of your autistic passions, totally immersed in the utter joy of it!

As an autist, we can feel the world and all that is around us deeply. Understanding your struggles plays such an important part in reframing your internal dialogue as different not difficult.

I hope the visual representation of this in your spiky profile will help you to develop a compassionate understanding of those immense highs and painful lows.

Changing the narrative around our struggles is a vital part of our autistic self-acceptance. From, 'Why am I so bad at this?' to, 'Ah, this is why I struggle and this is what I need help with.'

You are not difficult; this is what you are brilliant at! You are autistic and this is what you need to thrive.

CHAPTER 10

YOUR AUTISTIC FIRST AID KIT

The ultimate sign of autistic self-acceptance is learning to understand and take care of your needs.

Once you're able to do that, you can start to ask others to understand your struggles and ask for the adaptions you need to take care of yourself.

You might well be reading this and thinking, 'Pah! Load of self-indulgent nonsense. Self-care – we just have to get on with it, don't we?'

This is a key message we have receive from those who have gone before us – the post-war, baby boomer generation: 'You keep your head down and carry on!'

It's a message that's caused a mental health crisis – to be a successful human you must have... *resilience*! Plough on, regardless; do not indicate you are struggling or complain of any difficulty.

If reading this book and the wealth of information you have no doubt devoured as an autist haven't made this apparent... it takes a lot of energy for neurodivergent humans to navigate the demands of a 21st-century world.

Our challenges with sensory processing, experiencing and engaging with the world differently, which cause us to get dys-regulated, greatly affect our nervous system, and we are at much greater risk of mental and physical illness than neurotypical people.

In this chapter you'll get clarity on your autistic needs and the regular care you need to give yourself to stay healthy and well.

In our exploration of anxiety, overwhelm, meltdowns, shutdowns and burnout, we'll illuminate the signs that your tolerance levels have been exceeded to help you to realize that your 'battery' is in the red before it runs out completely.

This is to help you become aware of the signs that you are entering overwhelm and to understand a pattern to the triggers that can lead you into overwhelm.

There are lots of questions and activities to help you get clarity on the signs that you're experiencing difficulty and overwhelm and reflect on times that you have been in meltdown, shutdown or burnout. This will help you avoid the discomfort of regularly reaching those points.

This is all to help you become aware of the care you need to put in place for your needs – for your mind, body and soul – to help you regulate, protect your energy and design your Autist Care Instructions.

Anxiety

Anxiety is not exclusive to autists or neurodivergent folk, and maybe not all autists will experience high levels of anxiety.

A very large proportion of us do, however. Because of the alternative way we are wired, our sensory processing demands, a heightened alert system and the additional energy we need to adapt to ways of experiencing and communicating with the world, we are highly susceptible to anxiety.

In psychological terms, anxiety is defined as excessive apprehension about real or perceived threats.

In accepting myself as autistic, I have accepted that anxiety is part of my everyday life. Constantly thinking and wondering, 'Did I get it right? What will happen next?'

For me, life is eternally seeking peace, finding times when I can live in my natural rhythm without demands from others. I know there is no 'off switch' for the never-ending internal questions and responses to unexpected uncertainty, changes and a constantly evolving news cycle of high drama.

I now recognize this anxiety as one of the biggest signs of my undetected autism. It's astonishing really that I didn't realize how anxious I was before learning of my autism!

I'd absorbed all those labels I'd been given: a worrier, an overthinker, too sensitive.

Now that I recognize that anxiety is part of my autism, I do things every day that help me to manage it, to take care of it. I find ways to regulate myself, keeping anxiety to a low-level background hum.

If I don't do certain activities on a daily or weekly basis, my anxiety will, without doubt, get louder.

A build-up of uncertainty, an undefinable sense of dread or impending doom, going into the unknown, getting it wrong (whether this is real or perceived), making a mistake, unintentionally hurting someone – I recognize these as triggers. When they exceed my tolerance levels, especially if my energy levels are depleted, my anxiety *roars*!

This results in a heightened anxiety reaction of fight, flight, freeze or fawn (people pleasing):

- fight: a way of facing perceived threat aggressively
- flight: an urge to run from or avoid perceived danger
- freeze: an inability to move or act against threat
- fawn: a stress response to please someone to avoid conflict.

It can be debilitating at times. I can feel paralyzed with fear – I simply cannot move or carry out the simplest of tasks.

I have learned that I cannot push against this level of anxiety. It cannot be ignored or defeated, and as inconvenient as it can be, I have to surrender to it. This can be simply sitting with it – all the discomfort of it – and letting it fully take hold of me. When it grips me by the throat, it can be difficult to breathe, and once this part passes, I have to cry it out – just let the tears pour without having to explain or make sense of them.

I once worked with an amazing coach called Antony Parry. Before he started coaching, Antony was a journalist, often in places of high violence and war. He was born in the same year as David Bowie, whom we shared a love of. Antony is pretty kick-ass! He helped me to get out of my own way and stop being so bloody 'nice', as it was serving no one – especially not my clients, who needed to hear truthful insights and be questioned head-on about what they were avoiding.

In one of our coaching sessions, I had a mighty strong anxiety attack; it was paralyzing and I was struggling to breath. Antony didn't try to fix me or take the anxiety away. He sat on the other end of the phone and gently said, 'Surrender to it, don't fight it. Let the wave build and when it's crashed to shore, let's ask – what information is anxiety giving me?'

I still remember these wise words of Antony 'Yoda' master coach, some ten years on.

What information is anxiety giving you?

. . . .

. . . .

How does anxiety show up in you?

. . . .

. . . .

How frequently does anxiety feature in your life?

. . . .

. . . .

What triggers anxiety in you?

. . . .

. . . .

What categories or measures of anxiety work for you (e.g., I use 'hum' when it's a constant manageable background level and 'roar' when it's so overwhelming I feel paralyzed)?

. . . .

. . . .

What distinguishes the different categories (e.g., hum or roar) of anxiety you experience?

. . . .

. . . .

Meltdowns

When you cannot use the anxiety response of 'flight' to avoid or remove yourself from the overwhelming anxiety levels, you reach a heightened anxiety response of 'fight'.

I have experienced the most horrific meltdowns throughout my life. Once in action, there is *nothing* I can do to stop it, even when I hear my internal voice saying, 'What the fuck are you doing? Stop this now!'

If that quiet wise voice doesn't whisper to me mid-meltdown, it comes after the event, when I am wearily staggering from the meltdown scene, bewildered and utterly perplexed. 'What the hell just happened?' it will ask. I inwardly shrug and silently reply, 'If only I fucking knew!'

For without doubt, my meltdowns are 'drunken sailor' levels

of sweary. Swearing is actually joyful to me a lot of the time! When it's gone beyond a casual swear, when it's a torrent of swearing, it's a sure-fire sign that a melty is on its way or in action.

I read somewhere that when we are highly stressed, we cannot access the part of our brain that is connected to speech and language, so we take a shortcut to find words that can convey levels of emotion and stress quickly – nothing says I am in dangerous levels of fight or flight mode like 'Fuuuuuuuuuck!'

Many of us will have grown up with the message that in polite society ladies do not swear. This internalized bias adds to the shame post-meltdown.

Meltdowns are what happens to autistic people when they have reached a level of stress and overwhelm that they can simply no longer tolerate or deal with. A meltdown is an involuntary reaction that is designed to make the overwhelm stop – like an overheated engine that steams to release the unbearable pressure.

The reaction is strong and will vary for each individual. A common theme is the extremity of the reaction – a volatile eruption of such magnitude that will look to the standard passer-by, or meltdown witness/es, like a mighty temper tantrum – an eruption of pure white rage. Or it can be a torrent of uncontrollable crying – often judged as hysterical behaviour.

For some people, a meltdown can result in them wanting to push others away, so the reaction is physical. If that's an adult meltdown reaction, it can lead to the people involved retaliating or attempting to physically restrain you, and, given the overwhelm of your brain, nervous system and sensory processing, that is likely to further heighten your feeling of panic.

Whatever reaction you have during a meltdown, if it is in public or in the presence of others, there is one thing that almost certainly happens to you during and after the event – you are judged.

Volatile displays of emotion are not well tolerated within most societies. If your reality is at the intersection of bias, for example, if you are a black woman, the weight of judgement is even greater.

The shock of the meltdown creates shame in itself. Coupled with the weight of judgement from others, the shame is amplified to, at times, unbearable levels.

My meltdowns mostly happen in the comfort of my own home. I learned very early on in life that being a quiet sensible girl was praised and rewarded. 'She's no trouble,' I would often hear about myself when I was growing up.

This was not so if you shared a home with me. If you trashed my prized possessions (books) from the safe sanctuary of my bedroom, then I would most certainly respond in 'fight' mode, and if I was in total overwhelm, it would trigger me into a shouting meltdown rage. This was a key meltdown trigger for me.

'It's only a book!' they said. Ah, but it's not only a book, it's something that means the world to me in the only environment I can control, which brings me safety – my bedroom!

How do you experience meltdowns?

. . . .

. . . .

What triggers a meltdown in you (events, energy levels, etc.)?

. . . .

. . . .

Without doubt, hormones have a big part to play in meltdowns for me. I remember two horrifically shameful public occasions of hormone-induced meltdown.

As a 14- or 15-year-old teenager in puberty, who'd consumed the best part of a bottle of vodka at my first ever rave, I had a meltdown in panic that the friend I'd gone with had passed out. I thought she was going to die. We had not told our parents we were at this rave, and the endless possibility of having done something wrong and the danger took my levels of fear and tipped me into overwhelm. I started shouting and flailing my arms around, and as a result, was punched in the face by a not-so-impressed raver.

As a perimenopausal woman who had recently started HRT, I did not respond well to being told I could not go into the showing of a film I'd booked a ticket for because it was for mothers and babies only.

When I questioned why I was not allowed to go in, I was told I would make the babies feel unsafe... yes! I asked to speak to the manager! My line of questioning, whilst not abusive or sweary, was relentless. It felt incredibly unfair to be told I was excluded from the only screening I could get time to attend because I could make someone feel unsafe – especially a baby. The weight of that language and judgement of character triggered me into meltdown. Mid-meltdown, I was beyond logic.

I did hear that quiet voice in my head saying, 'Let it go, walk away.' Of course, these exhausted mothers deserved to watch the film in peace without the worry of being judged about their potentially howling babies.

I stumbled out of the cinema in a daze with my legs shaking and found myself getting lost on a street I know like the back of my hand. Afterwards, I was aghast that I'd had such an uncontrollable reaction. No, I have not been able to go back to that cinema.

Why am I sharing such shameful experiences with you? Because if we cannot get beyond our own embarrassment, which can feel acutely painful, we will never share our stories of something that is a part of the autistic experience and that needs to be understood.

Meltdowns are not reasonable; there is no logic or any use in being told to 'calm down!' (Does that ever work for anyone?!) They are difficult to experience and to witness. They are also powerful and mighty in the information they give.

The information is not, 'I am trying to be as difficult as possible.' The information is, 'I cannot cope. I am so overwhelmed I am reacting in this way to make it all stop.'

As an autist who feels the world deeply, I often have little control over tears. My eyes can fill up and tears can flow easily – in overwhelm at the beauty of something or in the sadness I feel at a situation or in sensing the difficulty and pain that others are experiencing.

The difference between those kinds of tears – everyday deep-feeling tears – and meltdown tears is that meltdown tears are uncontrollable. They are deep belly sobs – river-bursting levels that cannot be stopped.

A natural human reaction to seeing a person cry is to try and comfort them.

Human touch or closeness during a meltdown is just too much. I am in a state of total overwhelm, nervous system and processing overload. I cannot deal with processing close human touch in these moments.

This can be perceived as a coldness or pushing someone away. I already feel overwhelming levels of bewilderment and shame from the meltdown, and now I have to contend with the guilt and shame about your feeling of rejection!

Likewise, the caring human that looks at you aghast and asks, 'What can I do to help?!' It's almost impossible to answer this caring question – you are beyond knowing what you need, your brain is completely out of control. Whilst you'd love to growl, 'Fuck off!', like *Succession*'s Logan Roy, what can tend to happen towards the crescendo of meltdown is that you can no longer speak.

What I find helpful is the safety of quiet room where I can either just stare into space or lie still until I can regulate myself again. Sometimes I need to shut down completely, and once regulated, I close my eyes until I can move again.

What helps you to recover from a meltdown?

. . . .

. . . .

Meltdown Warning Signs

Sometimes there is no avoiding a meltdown. It is a necessary, albeit deeply uncomfortable, way to inform you that you are in overwhelm, especially if you are unaware of it or chose to ignore the warning signs.

Since accepting I'm autistic, I have started to become aware of the warning signs that I am entering a dangerous level of overwhelm and potentially about to enter meltdown territory.

All of my warning signs are physical...

I want to pull my hair out! Every tiny part of my body feels irritated, but a definite warning sign is when my hair is irritating me to such a degree that I literally want to pull it out!

I feel fizzy. My whole body feels like it's unsettled and like I've been picked up and repeatedly shaken.

My clothes feel wrong! In fact *everything* feels wrong and it's all deeply irritating.

The only other warning sign is in my heightened stress reactions. My reactions and physical experience become more panicky. This can be difficult to differentiate from an anxiety roar for me; the only distinguishing feature is in the outcome: anxiety attack or meltdown!

What are your meltdown warning signs?

. . . .

. . . .

There are ways you can minimize the risk of a meltdown, and that will form a key part of you designing your own Autist Care Instructions.

However, whilst we can understand or own meltdowns – how they feel, what they are in response to and the warning signs – we can't eradicate them from our lives completely, and neither should we.

Meltdowns inform us that we need to take care of ourselves, ask for help, make adaptions or consider adjustments we can make.

Shutdowns

Shutdowns are the extreme anxiety response of 'freeze'.

Whilst in shutdown, you can be robbed of the power of speech or be unable to form coherent and understandable sentences.

I can be completely immobilized.

Sometimes shutdowns come after a meltdown, or they can happen alone.

I've had a shutdown in times of heightened conflict or when my anxiety is too much to navigate.

Like meltdowns, they are deeply uncomfortable and often inexplicable. It is difficult for those around you to understand or know what to do – especially as you cannot find or speak words.

They might assume you're ignoring them or being difficult. During a shutdown, the information you receive or give is minimal. All of your senses shut down. It can cause you to be mute; you may have a blank expression or appear frozen. This can make you unreachable to others and vice versa.

Shutdowns can render you immobile. Whilst your discomfort may be less obvious than during a meltdown, internally it can feel like total defeat and withdrawal. I can feel panicky inside when I can't form words or move. I have wondered, during one bout of shutdown, if I was having a nervous breakdown.

Shutdowns require a level of awareness and understanding from you and those around you. In understanding that your body and mind need stillness and silence to regulate, you can remove the fear or burden of explanation. It will be helpful if those around you accept and understand that you can't communicate during these times and this time of stillness and silence, of no input, is required for you to regulate your mind, body and nervous system to resume interaction.

I have at times reached a level of overwhelm where I simply

have to shut down to regulate. A shutdown is a bit of a reboot for the overwhelmed autist's mind and body.

How do you experience shutdown?

. . . .

. . . .

What are your shutdown warning signs?

. . . .

. . . .

What triggers a shutdown in you?

. . . .

. . . .

Your Energy Bank Account

A simple and significant way to take care of your autistic self is to recognize what takes up a lot of your energy.

Once you accept your own difference, you can understand that you can choose to do social interaction, and yes, it will take you a lot more energy than a neurotypical human.

You can even take to a stage to tell your story or perform, host or take part in panel discussions to change perceptions of what autism is and the changes we need. The energy it takes will need to be replenished, and you will need time to recover from the things that take a lot of energy from you.

This means you will need to make choices about what you say yes to and what you say no to, because – and this is very important for me to emphasize here – you *do* get to choose.

Accepting yourself as autistic means that you no longer need to please all of the people all of the time. No, that doesn't make you a bad person. It makes you a person who values yourself, your health, your wellbeing and the quality of the life you live.

Choosing what you say yes to and what you say no to might mean you need to ask others for their support in adapting or adjusting environments and events. Or you might simply need to ask for their understanding, for example, 'This is too much for me right now,' or 'I can come for an hour and I will need to leave when I'm done.'

This is the fundamental part of taking care of yourself: managing and protecting your energy.

Spending time considering this will really benefit you in getting clear on how that looks for you on a daily, weekly and monthly basis.

I think you'll be pleasantly surprised by how simple some of this is! It doesn't mean you have to overhaul your entire life; it just means you have to replace what energy you use before it gets used up, leaving your overwhelm to reach excessive and damaging levels.

Understanding what takes and gives you energy can help you to plan in recovery time after you've done something that takes a lot of energy from you. Think of it as your energy bank account – you need to keep it balanced.

YOUR ENERGY ECONOMY

In the space below, write down all the activities you do regularly, have coming up or would really like to do.

. . . .

. . . .

. . . .

. . . .

. . . .

. . . .

. . . .

. . . .

Consider the following questions:

- Before: How much energy will it take to prepare for each activity? (If it helps, think of your energy in percentages.)
- During: How much energy will it take to do each activity?
- After: How long will it take you to recover from these activities?
- What generates energy for you? (E.g., a project or task you love doing, being in nature, writing, listening to music, going for a walk, etc.)
- How important is rest to you? What forms can rest take – as well as the obvious example of sleep, what else rests your nervous system, mind and body?

Use the following table to list all the activities that cost you energy and all the activities that will replenish the energy you use.

Energy cost		Energy saving	

When you look at these lists, what are you struck by?

. . . .

. . . .

Are they balanced?

. . . .

. . . .

Are you allowing yourself time to recover?

. . . .

. . . .

Are you surprised by how much energy it takes to do some of the activities?

. . . .

. . . .

What changes can you make to where your energy is spent?

. . . .

. . . .

Write down below what you want to say yes and no to. And write down anything that you want to ask to be adapted or adjusted to make it less draining for you.

Yes	No	Adaptions

Autist Care Instructions

Taking your energy economy to the next level, we're going to look at what your Autist Care Instructions would look like for you.

This will help you consciously consider and actively plan all the things you can do to maintain a level of care that will help you navigate the additional challenges you have as an autist, so you can experience and engage with the world in a way that makes you feel well and fulfilled. Think about the following questions.

- **Mind:** What helps you to make sense of yourself and your internal world?
- **Emotions:** What helps you to make sense of and connect with your feelings?
- **Body:** What helps you to feel grounded, peaceful or connected to something bigger than you?
- **Rest:** What helps you to relax and rest? What helps you to sleep well?
- **Nourishment:** What food makes you feel good and gives you a good release of energy?

There are activities I need to do daily to help me manage my anxiety; writing 'morning pages' (from Julia Cameron Artist's Way book/course) has been life-changing for me. Writing three pages of an unconscious stream of what's in my head massively helps me to make sense of how I am feeling, what underlying anxiety there might be and the ideas that are floating in my head.

Some things need to happen weekly, like yoga, running and going for a walk to happy places. I have certain treatments once a month to try and maintain my body, because I really struggle to connect with any pain I might be holding in my body or even to connect my body and mind together at all.

I know that these are the things that form my care instructions. If I don't maintain them on a regular basis, my anxiety roars, I have more regular meltdowns and I head towards burn-out, and then it takes a lot more time to get through recovery.

Below is a space for you to design your own Autist Care Instructions. If you give it a go, experiment with it for a month or two and then come back to adjust it based on what worked.

AUTIST CARE INSTRUCTIONS

	Activity	When	Frequency
Mind			
Emotions			
Body			
Energy			
Rest			
Nourishment			

If you do not make time for your wellness, you will be forced to make time for your illness.

I'm sure that, like me, you see that quote bandied around on social media on a regular basis. The #readthatagain hashtag did its job of making me pause and really take it in. It's a powerful quote and worth contemplating.

This leads me to the final part of this chapter: burnout.

Burnout

In 2019, the World Health Organization (WHO) officially recognized burnout as an occupational phenomenon. That phenomenon has been amplified during the COVID pandemic in which the lines between life and work have become blurred, with many of us working in our homes, often whilst being expected to school our children and provide healthcare for seriously ill family members.

Burnout is defined as physical and mental exhaustion that occurs when you experience long-term stress.

Burnout can result in insomnia and a loss of motivation and compassion for the things and people you love. Plus loss of confidence, procrastination, crying, loss of concentration, physical illness... the list goes on and on.

Autistic burnout is defined as chronic exhaustion, chronic life stress and a mismatch of expectations and abilities without adequate support. It involves pervasive long-term (three months plus) exhaustion, loss of function and reduced tolerance to stimulus.

I discuss some of the factors specific to autistic burnout below.

Cause

Burnout can be caused by long-term stress, normally from work or from the emotional burden that can be carried as a caregiver

– especially given what we all lived through during the global pandemic.

Autistic burnout can be caused by the pressures of living and heavily masking in a neurotypical world, where sensory and social overload become intolerable.

Anxiety Response (Fawn) and Lifelong People Pleasing

We may continue to work and perform during burnout as we are so used to our automatic anxiety response of fawn that we feel we must keep on pleasing people. We become frightened to show our struggles for fear of being selfish or unreliable. We can't bear to think that we may let people down if we do not deliver in line with their expectations. We are so addicted to the validation of being considered valuable to others in what we achieve that we cannot stop – not even when our burned-out body and mind are begging for a rest.

Struggles with Interoception

As autists we can struggle with interoception, which is the sense that helps us to connect with our bodily needs, for example, identifying hunger, temperature and pain – and even whether we need to go to the toilet.

This makes self-regulation a challenge for us. In the context of illness and burnout, we may not be able to identify how exhausted we are until it's too late.

We Don't Realize We're Running on Empty

All of us late-discovered autists became used to being a state of high stress at an early age, probably from the point when we started school.

This high stress, hypervigilance and anxiety is the way we live every day due to the increased sensory processing and social challenges and demands placed on us, and we have been without information and support for these challenges for our entire lives. We normalize this stress, seeing it as 'life': this is just what it takes to live this life!

It is not normal! And neither should we normalize or dismiss burnout and autistic burnout as being an expected way to live.

Fool that I am, I was hopeful, especially during that very first lockdown in the pandemic, that this enforced pause would help us all to slow down and change our expectations for how we work, rest and play.

It showed that we can indeed work flexibly and can be trusted to work in ways that work for us.

There has been a shift for most of us in our consciousness in how we value nature and community. The 'Big Resignation' post-pandemic did not happen by accident. Many of us just did not want to carry on working at one million miles an hour.

The old guard are determined to drag us back to the good old pre-pandemic days. We're going through a shift, and we haven't come out the other side yet. Economic and climate crises and many other emergencies make it difficult to see how it will ever change.

Regardless of the tumultuous world we live in, you, dear reader, have a choice in how much you value your health and the quality of life you want to live.

Remember... if you do not make time for your wellness, you will be forced to make time for your illness.

Recovery

The final distinction between burnout and autistic burnout is what will help you during recovery.

When you're in autistic burnout, your reduced tolerance to stimuli will mean that some of the classic things that help with burnout, such as time with friends, walks and time in nature, can be unbearable in recovery. This means your recovery plan will need to be adapted to tune into that.

Your Recovery Plan

If you're in autistic burnout, you should be doing very little activity at all – the bare minimum.

As a parent, I fully know and understand that if you have dependants, you cannot simply stop caring for them.

The harsh reality is this: you will not recover from burnout if you do not take time to rest.

That's likely to mean you will be unable to work until you have recovered and are well enough to be able to function fully. You need to retreat, shut down the outside world and rest as fully as you possibly can.

The following activity gives an outline of what that recovery might look like for you. It will help you to consider what things will support you to get into recovery mode and the changes you might need to make to stay recovered – to avoid repetition of burnout, which is sure to lead to more serious illness.

In truth, this is also written for any family members or loved ones of a late-discovered autist – because your understanding of the damage of autistic burnout is really important. You need to look out for the signs and be prepared to adapt and adjust to help your loved one.

From my own experience of autistic burnout, I was beyond reading a book once I'd reached this stage. I was so desperate for those around me to understand how much I was struggling. I was really scared and I did not have the words to explain any of this. How can anyone in autistic burnout really have what's needed to explain? They are chronically exhausted!

Due to excessive periods of running on adrenaline and your body and mind being in continuous stress, sleep may be really difficult for you. The first part of recovery is recalibrating your nervous system enough that your sleep pattern improves.

RECOVERY PLAN

Use the table below to write down your thoughts and actions for your recovery plan.

	Your thoughts and actions

Stop
Focus on recalibrating your nervous system.
 	
· Quiet:
  – Where's the most peaceful place for you in the home?
 	
· Rest:
  – Where's the most relaxing place you can rest at home?
  – What will it take to have complete rest?
  – Can anyone help you with caring for dependants?
 	
· Digital detox:
  – Who can you give your phone to so they can manage messages or calls to give you peace?
  – Can you let essential people know you are switching your phone off?
 	
· Comforting food:
  – What food you can tolerate?
 	
· Cleanse:
  – What cleansing rituals can you tolerate – bathe in Epsom salts, calming cleansers?	

cont.

	Your thoughts and actions
Start Gently introduce stimuli that you love. If your senses can't tolerate it, don't push it – go back to **stop**. · Be in nature. · Watch films or programmes you love. · Listen to music you love. · Write – journal or spend time each morning or evening writing as little or as much as you can about what's inside your head. · Movement: What movement do you love? How can you gently introduce it? Asking for help: · Who can help you emotionally? · Who can help you practically? · Who can provide you with the nutrients that might help to energize you? · Do you have a specialist/ healthcare practitioner? · Do you have disability support? Considering the changes you or others need to make: · Adjustments – small alterations to meet your needs. · Adaptions – aligned with the purpose of keeping you well. · Accommodations – a change to arrangements.	
Continue Re-evaluate and follow your Autist Care Instructions.	

You might have received messages throughout your entire life that it's self-indulgent to look after yourself.

Caring about your mind, your body, even considering yourself spiritually... 'Who do you think you are? Lady Muck?!'

Your nervous system operates on high alert most of the time, and more than anything you may want to be considered valuable and helpful and to just fit in like everyone else – you might be desperate to get it right.

You haven't known or understood why some things in life are so challenging and stressful for you.

You do now. You're autistic. You're different, not difficult. Your differences are not a deficit.

Those who choose to see autism in those narrow deficit-based ways that make us feel defective and marginalize us are creating lasting damage – for you as a human, who has received the message that 'there's something wrong with you, and us collectively'.

It's time to heal from all of that damage.

You're equipped with the information you need to be understanding about and have compassion for your needs. The ultimate self-acceptance of being autistic is caring for yourself and asking others to understand your needs.

If you've got children or young people that matter to you in life, changing your patterns and showing them that taking care of yourself and your health is important will have a lasting impact on them and how they live their life.

If you've taken the time to consider any of the questions in this chapter about anxiety, meltdowns, shutdowns and burnout, I applaud you.

If you've taken the time to do any of the activities to help you consider and act upon ways you can live in balance, I hope they help you to form regular habits that will help you stay well.

I don't find this stuff easy myself! When I'm dysregulated or my energy is low, I feel guilty about writing my morning pages, even though I know they are essential to managing my anxiety in the day ahead.

I am slow to start in the morning and I hear self-sabotaging voices of doubt creeping in sometimes, 'You should get up earlier, you're so lazy!'

I have a ritual where I put my right hand on my left shoulder as a symbol of comfort. 'You're alright sweetheart!' I say inside my head.

Because one of the biggest lessons I've learned in accepting myself as autistic is that it's time to have a kinder internal dialogue with myself. Hold on to your hats... I'm going in for the L word! I have learned to love myself, autism and all!

I hope you do the same for yourself too.

CHAPTER 11

ABLEISM: A LIFE UNLIMITED?

When I first started writing this book, one year after my own late-life autism discovery, this chapter was about how our strengths, some of which are shaped by our autism, can help us to thrive.

Some of us find it easier to seek out and be welcomed into environments where we can thrive than others. And this brings me to how my thinking and writing have evolved, and what this chapter has developed into. For all lives are not unlimited. I've finally had my eyes opened. In fully accepting I am autistic, I've had to consider the question: am I disabled? Is my autism a disability?

I have also, in the course of my work in hosting talks about creating environments for neurodivergent folk to thrive, had the joy of being introduced to some amazing people who have helped me to see that we do not all have the same starting point.

Culture and class give some of us a privileged starting point – a shortcut into places that other people can't even find the door for.

In some cultures, there is no word, language or term that describes autism or neurodivergence.

Many autistic and neurodivergent folk are at an intersection of disadvantage based on the circumstances that they are born into. Their place in society is dictated by rules, hierarchies and social structures created by white cis males, who do all they can to create systems and barriers to keep themselves in positions of power that dictate the shape of the lives we live.

For all my lifelong belief in social justice and treating everybody equally, I can clearly see that equity trumps equality in what we really need to help everyone to thrive.

Equity is only reached when we all have the same starting point.

This chapter is about autistic ableism.

My own self-limiting ableist beliefs will come into play here. I will be brutally honest (i.e., autistic!), as I am in all aspects of this book, about my discomfort in my own limited views and all the questions it continues to throw up for me as I get curious and want to learn and grow in my understanding.

I don't feel disabled. I am autistic and I do not feel disabled by that. My life has been unlimited by autism – that's because as a white, middle-class woman, it's a privilege to proudly share, 'I'm autistic,' and whilst I experience some discomfort at the judgement I get from some people in my life, there is no real threat to my safety or comfort.

There are questions for you along the way in this chapter to provoke deeper thought and to illuminate any unconscious bias that is creating a barrier to you accepting yourself as autistic.

A big part of accepting yourself as autistic is an honest exploration into the societal opinions and your own conditioning that can influence limiting beliefs.

Considering your own thoughts and beliefs around disability and whether you consider autism to be a disability, or autistic people to be disabled people, is an important part of how you identify with autism and whether that affects the ease with which you are open in your neurodivergence.

In this chapter we'll explore the intersections of disadvantage. 'Intersectionality' is a term coined by Kimberlé Williams Crenshaw meaning overlapping or intersecting social identities and related systems of domination, oppression or discrimination.

What's the Difference between Disabled and Disability?

The roots of this distinction can be found in the two different and opposing models that shape the attitudes, behaviour and treatment of those with visible or invisible differences and affect how they experience and live their lives.

Medical Model

In the medical model, the attitude is that the person has an impairment that causes them to have an inability to participate or access goods and services.

Disability very much sits within this medical model of deficit and deficiency in relation to 'the norm'.

Putting it crudely, the belief within this model is that the person with an impairment is a problem. The person with an impairment needs to be fixed. The person with an impairment needs a special service designed for them, and that person with an impairment is going to cost us – the people without an impairment – money.

Assumptions about the person with an impairment – a disability – are made in relation to their capabilities and needs without a dialogue with them.

Disability costs 'The Man' money. This does not sit well in a capitalist system where time is money, and efficiency and productivity are the master.

The headline of this medical model is: if you have a disability, you can't make a meaningful contribution in society because the main measures are achievement, productivity and capital output.

The biggest barrier that is created by the medical model is in the use of it to inform and develop the structure of legislation. It's by this tool – the law – that institutions and corporations stretch their muscles. They often do the bare minimum to meet legal requirements that mostly create barriers for those who diverge from the 'typical'.

Is Autism a Disability?

For those in employment in the UK, through the medical model of disability and its accompanying legislation, autism is likely to be considered a disability under the Equality Act 2010. This is because autistic people face difficulties in certain areas of life, such as sensory and verbal processing, along with differences in how we communicate and socially interact, all of which are involved in normal day-to-day activities. This means employers have an obligation to make reasonable adjustments.

This is all well and good, assuming you can get your foot in the door and through application processes riddled with barriers and prejudice.

Assuming you're able to 'mask' enough to comply with the myriad unspoken cultural social rules to be employed permanently within a business, you then have to contend with the overly formal need to disclose your late-life neurodivergence discovery or diagnosis.

The burden of that huge emotionally challenging task might be all the more complex if you work within an environment in which it is not psychologically safe to be seen as different.

What associations are you making with the medical model of disability?

. . . .

. . . .

Social Model

The social model states that it is the barriers imposed by systems that have been put in place that disable and prevent full participation in society and the ability to access work and live independently.

In this model, people with physical or mental differences do not have a disability but it's something that is experienced as a result of barriers and exclusions imposed upon them.

Unsurprisingly, the social model was created by disabled people. It began around the 1970s in disability rights movements.

This model is about identifying and removing systemic barriers. This includes redesigning environments, systems and products so that they are accessible to everyone.

There are clear benefits for everyone of doing this, not just those who are disabled by existing services and systems. An example of this is audiobooks. Their initial creation was of benefit to those with a visual impairment, and they have benefited everyone, worldwide.

Another example is drop kerbs: kerbs that are lowered to allow wheelchair access, which have provided additional benefits for pushchair and bike access.

Of course, altering the access, removing barriers for everyone... well, that takes a lot more consideration in terms of design and time to consult with those who need the alterations the most – and time is the master of capitalism!

Arguably, creating 'special' services, as happens in the medical model, is a false economy and will always end up costing more. These special services can be undignified for the user and can further exclude people with additional needs.

The social model requires more thought, consideration and engagement with those who need the barriers removed – to ask them about their experiences and needs, and to really understand the barriers that prevent them from inclusion.

In the first episode of Poppy Field's excellent podcast, 'Call Me Disabled', she is in conversation with Jameisha Prescod about disabled identity and radical resting.

Jameisha talks about how it felt empowering for her to claim 'disabled' as part as her identity. For her, it felt like this was not about her chronic illness but about recognizing that she is disabled because of the barriers put in place to exclude her and to stop her thriving in certain places.

For Jameisha, the disabled movement is about speaking out about the politics of disability and how capitalism heaps shame on all of us if we don't meet the 'success criteria' in how much we contribute.

In this context, taking the rest your body and mind needs can be a radical act – for all of us, not only those who are disabled by the systemic barriers imposed.

What associations are you making with the social model of disability?

. . . .

. . . .

Unconscious Bias

Unconscious bias is the judgements we make about people based on unconscious thoughts or feelings.

Our unconscious bias can be influenced by the stories we're told in education, by family, friends and in messages we get from media.

What stories have you always been told about people who are different?

. . . .

. . . .

What stories did you grow up hearing about mental illness?

. . . .

. . . .

What stories did you hear about people who were different beyond your family?

. . . .

. . . .

What has been the biggest influence on shaping your thinking about people who stand out as different?

. . . .

. . . .

What Is Ableism?

Abelism is discrimination of and social prejudice in favour of non-disabled people. It is based on the belief that 'typical' abilities are superior.

Like racism and sexism, ableism classifies entire groups of people as 'less than'. It generalizes and includes harmful stereotypes and misconceptions about the strengths and needs of those with physical and mental differences.

This can show up for us in the internal dialogue we have with ourselves when we disregard our own needs, for example, 'There's people worse off than me.'

It was my own ableism that prevented me from allowing myself to consider that my son is autistic. Removing that barrier from my mind in putting his needs ahead of my own fear of him, or me, being different, 'less than', has allowed our whole worlds to open up to new possibilities and ways of acknowledging and addressing our needs.

Without doubt, I have a long way to go in my thinking and contribution to this discussion, to join my voice to a collective movement for positive change in the removal of barriers that exist for one fifth of the world's population.

Prejudice + Power = Ableism

Power is held by the dominant culture, and where you sit in relation to the dominant culture will shape your social identity.

Your privilege comes from where you hold power and agency – the benefits you receive based on how aligned you are to the dominant culture.

What privilege do you hold?

. . . .

. . . .

Check Your Privilege!

Here it comes... my cringey discomfort!

I might've considered myself fully in acceptance of being autistic and feeling okay about publicly posting or commenting on social media, proudly owning my autism.

This doesn't make me exempt from reminders about the privilege allowed to me by my class and culture, and I hope it never does.

Emboldened by my autistic, neurodivergent and proud status! I took offence to an advert on social media proclaiming to rid the consumer of all 'ADHD symptoms'. The product was a mushroom tea, the mushroom being lion's mane.

I'd seen this particular advert on my feed repeatedly: 'It gets rid of ADHD symptoms!' and 'If you suffer with ADHD this will get rid of your symptoms!' It got under my skin, and after one time too many of seeing it, I decided to post a comment: 'ADHD is not an illness!' So said I, and on I rambled about 'symptoms' inferring that neurodivergence was an illness, and then I got indignant and self-righteous: 'Please seek input from the neurodivergent community before advertising these products!'

Given the extent of the anxiety I experience from any active participation in social media, making such a comment on an advert that anyone could see... well, this was quite out of character!

What followed was a stark reminder to me to check my privilege!

To start with I got the dopamine hit of many people liking my comment. Such was the number of likes that it seemed to be shown as the top comment on the advert for a while.

Then the sheen wore off and dopamine was spent, and anxiety surges took the place of dopamine. 'No one said ADHD was an illness. I suffer with ADHD it makes my life difficult every day,' was the first reply my comment received.

I get a sort of gut-punch anxiety – that rising heat and prickly sensation – when the 'I've done something wrong' trigger takes hold. A collision of fear, shame and panic takes control of me and I am paralyzed – frozen as all this weird physical sensation is taking hold of my brain.

I took a deep breath and thought, 'No, I am not going to back down.'

And policing language and rigid gatekeeping can be damaging at the early stage of neurodivergent awareness and mainstream discussion. When we're quick to police language at this stage, it can get defences up, create shame and close down progress being made in neurodivergence being widely understood.

So, I very thoughtfully responded to the comment: 'It's quite unlike me to comment on an advert, I took offence to the inference of ADHD being an illness in the use of words like suffer and symptoms. I also do not like the commodification of neurodivergence for products claiming to remove the effects of it...'

And this response was met with a very considered response and we actually had a very positive conversation about our opposing views.

I could breathe deeply and calmly again... until the next comment came.

This next one, well, it was the thing that really made me realize that my own unconscious bias was creating self-limiting and judgemental ableist views: 'Please be more considerate in your comments and do not diminish the struggles I and others live with, physically and mentally every day. As a result of my ADHD. I cannot work and my son cannot go to school.'

I thanked the woman who wrote that. We grow from discomfort, as I certainly did with this incident! A big part of that growth is acknowledging our mistakes.

For yes, here I am... autistic, and for sure, this impacts on my mental health mostly – anxiety can be crippling for me at times. I get physically unwell and exhausted, burnt out. And I have the provisions and resources to work around this until I can get well again.

Who am I to assume that everyone has this available to them? Autism and neurodivergence can completely alter the quality of lives.

Intersectionality

Quality of life is affected most for those at the intersections of disadvantage in age, gender, sexual preference, social-economic class, ethnicity and of course neurodivergence.

Every time I hear Atif Choudhury, CEO and co-founder of Diversity and Ability, hosting or taking part in a discussion about neurodiversity, I learn something new, often something uncomfortable and thought-provoking.

In a talk on culture, community and class that Atif hosted as part of Neurodiversity Celebration Week, it was illuminated how much neurodivergence is intertwined in intersectionality.

The negative narratives we are fed originate at these points of intertwined intersectionality, for example, the untrue narrative that 'black women are aggressive'. This is how silos for exclusion are created.

In order for us to find liberation from those who hold the power of our treatment, there needs to be space for those intersectional stories to be told and embraced in order for the label of neurodivergence to become collectively powered.

In talking with Marsha Martin, founder of Black SEN Mamas UK, about how exhausting masking is for those within that community – black mothers and sole carers of SEND (special educational needs and disabilities)/neurodivergent children – she illuminated how difficult it is to challenge education systems when they are failing your children.

'I can't tell them I'm autistic,' she said, when I asked her to share more about the internal narrative she carries and why she has to mask her autism:

> Well, they will just label me difficult to deal with if I tell them I'm autistic. They already tell me I'm aggressive when I question why my child is not getting the provisions that have been agreed with them. I'm not being aggressive! My child's health and education matter to me, I am being passionate in expressing that and I am told 'I am finding you aggressive!'

Marsha shared with me that neurodivergence is not openly talked about within the black community. The women within Black SEN Mamas are having to mask their own difference within not only the education system but also their own cultures, where the pressure to compensate and pull *all* the stops out – the pressure to be a strong black woman – is heightening those masking challenges even more.

How do we get to a place where we show up for the others who are disadvantaged? We grow from our discomfort. It starts with acknowledging our mistakes. We listen carefully to help us consider our own unconscious bias.

What mistakes have you made in your bias or unconscious bias in ableism?

. . . .

. . . .

> What can you do differently to grow from it?
>
> . . . .
>
> . . . .

Where Do I Belong ?

A big part of accepting yourself as autistic is moving beyond fitting in, moving beyond surviving and doing what's necessary to comply with a mould that is not designed for you.

When we start to question what belonging will really look like for us, when we are able to safely show up as our true selves, we can consider what power and agency we have individually.

Along with the consideration of neurodivergent people beyond our communities – who are disadvantaged, who really struggle – we can consider how we can use our power to change perceived normality – to remove barriers.

> How can you use your privilege to disrupt ableism?
>
> . . . .
>
> . . . .

I want to acknowledge that it is not easy to look at any bias or unconscious bias we hold and how that can affect the way we communicate and behave; in fact, it's really uncomfortable.

That is exactly where our growth comes from – we grow from discomfort.

Awareness is always the first part of our growth. When we can make space in our lives for honest reflection or to 'look in the mirror' at who we truly are – how our own thoughts and behaviours are preventing us from embracing our own difference – that's when we are able to change the internal dialogue.

Evolving our own thinking about how we see ourselves, when we can acknowledge how our mistakes or self-limiting beliefs are getting in the way of positive change – that's when we can start to consciously choose how we are going to act or behave differently.

This place creates more choices for us. Not all of those choices are easy ones, but they are all new possibilities.

One of the things I love about being autistic is my endless curiosity and desire to keep learning and growing. There is no finish line or final destination. This learning life malarkey... well, it's lifelong!

When you give yourself permission to be a learner at life it frees you up to be okay with making mistakes and never being right. If that's you – congratulations!

Enjoy the expansion that will come when you keep on talking to people outside the reach of your culture, class and social identity.

It's okay to ask, 'What's this like for you?', 'What are the barriers to you being welcomed in?' and 'What can I do to help remove those barriers?'

CHAPTER 12

AUTISTIC ACCEPTANCE: APPLY WITHIN

Looking for External Acceptance and Finding It Within

For a long, long time – a lifetime in fact! – I was looking for acceptance from others.

This also applied to my autism discovery. For much of my dance from autism awareness to accepting myself as autistic was about looking for signs that me being autistic was accepted by others.

As a late-discovered autist, it's a big ask for a family that's known you for 30, 40, 50, even 60 years to accept you in a way that they perhaps don't fully understand.

The genetic link with neurodivergence can make sharing your autism discovery a complicated thing to discuss with your family. You may also be carrying the hope of acceptance within a family you've always felt misunderstood by.

Generational differences mean that expectations around acceptable behaviour have changed over the years.

I grew up in an era where children were 'seen and not heard'. You were praised for sitting quietly and replying politely to your elders, who were also your betters.

Aligned with what distinguishes the generation that came after ours, my children are being raised differently to how I was raised. We encourage them to speak for themselves and ask questions, and we don't expect them to sit like statues in silence in places they find boring, such as restaurants, or at social gatherings.

As you've supported and understood your child's neurodivergence, their differences may be more pronounced than yours. You've been masking your own difference your entire life, so it may not be so obvious... yet.

The generation before yours might support and understand the neurodivergence in your child and want them to get access to the best support possible.

You? Of course you're not autistic! How can you be – look at all you've achieved! Nothing wrong with you! Of course, they should know – they brought you up!

In essence, this chapter is about getting to a place where you recognize that the acceptance you've been seeking is not going to come in the way you, perhaps, initially wanted it to.

You can find the acceptance you need from yourself.

You know what matters most to you, what your strengths are and why you find some things challenging or difficult. You've learned what your own needs are and what helps you to take care of yourself and your needs. That's a core part of accepting you're autistic.

In this chapter we'll look at three levels of acceptance:

Self: 'I'm Autistic'	What you acknowledge and celebrate in your own autistic self-acceptance.
Others: Protect	Those who cannot accept us for who we truly are. Those who choose not to see us as autistic. With these people, we need to accept the things we cannot change and consider how best to protect ourselves around them.
Others: Belong	Those who accept and embrace us as autistic. We feel an affinity and belonging with these people.

We'll acknowledge that part of this process is grieving and letting go of old stories and perspectives that no longer serve us.

The aim of doing this is to mark a new relationship with ourselves and a change in how we choose to relate to others – those who choose not to accept us as autistic and those who do.

Mostly, we'll spend time acknowledging and celebrating you and how much you've grown in this exploration of autism and you.

 It's taken a lot of courage to arrive here – at this place where you accept you're autistic. You've had to navigate a lot of discomfort, to curiously dig in and ask some big questions of yourself and your life.

This process has illuminated what brings you joy and makes you feel alive, and it's required you to re-examine difficult aspects of your life with new information.

Self-acceptance is an important milestone to be acknowledged and celebrated, a positive turning point that you have created.

It marks a changed relationship with ourselves; we are kinder to ourselves in self-acceptance.

It can also mark a change in how we relate to others. Reaching autistic acceptance can become the beginning of belonging, rather than shrinking and moulding yourself to fit.

In understanding and knowing there are others out there who experience the world as we do, we feel less isolated and alone. And that gives us choices in how we want to show up and with whom.

Letting Go

A large part of this process of getting to self-acceptance has been about shedding and letting go.

Before you were aware of autism – autism and you – you had a sense of self and an image of who you are and how you are experienced by others.

Whatever your turning point – the realization that you are different, that maybe autism is a part of you – in that moment, you started letting go. Letting go of a belief of who you are.

For any change or transformation to happen, we need to make space for the newness to come in. We can't keep all the old stuff, the old stories, the old beliefs and expect the new stuff to have enough space to grow.

When you had all the doubts of, 'Can I really be autistic? I am totally imagining this!', it was really about the fear of letting go of the safety of the old familiar stuff.

For all of us, going into the unknown can be scary. For us autists who quite like to be prepared, we like to have as much certainty as possible – it regulates us. This makes going into the unknown even more fraught!

Here's the thing... we're still the same people. You don't completely change when you accept you're autistic. In essence, you're still the same person; you just have new information and a deeper level of understanding about yourself.

The freedom comes in allowing ourselves to be authentic. We can actually show the world who we really are. Feeling beyond bewildered and exhausted from trying to fit ourselves to a mould not made for us, exhausting ourselves in pleasing others and not taking care of our own needs – that is what we are letting go of.

What are you letting go of?

. . . .

. . . .

What grudges and fears are you letting go of?

. . . .

. . . .

Help Me to Change What I Cannot Accept and Accept What I Cannot Change

This is a phrase that sticks in my mind. It's a paraphrase of the serenity prayer: 'Grant me the serenity to accept the things I cannot change, the courage to change the things I can and the wisdom to know the difference.'

The paraphrase or the whole serenity prayer will apply to you freeing yourself from the burden of waiting for friends or family who do not accept you as autistic to come round to your way of thinking!

This has perhaps been one of the most difficult things for me to navigate in getting to acceptance of being autistic.

I feel it – the internal or the actual eye-roll that allistic friends give me when I talk about being autistic. At times I do feel like the character in the film *American Pie*, who repeatedly says, 'This one time, at band camp...'.

It's part of being autistic – for me, autism has become a passion... a 'special interest'. And I know enough about social niceties to know that it can't be the only topic of our conversation, at least not with these friends.

I have found my neurodivergent people – the ones who also share the passion of being a late-discovered neurodivergent – and we can talk together about all the intricacies of being neurodivergent without constraint!

Sometimes that acceptance, inclusion, welcoming and belonging won't come naturally into the places we were born into or be there in the ways we want it to be. We cannot expect others to do the work they don't want to do.

That is difficult to accept.

There is a cost, which is that these people will never have the joy of knowing the real you, the authentic one you've been searching your whole life to find. It's a sad thing – you can acknowledge that sadness and choose to let that expectation go.

You can choose to accept the things you cannot change.

You can, of course, choose not to have these people in your life anymore.

If you do choose to keep them included in part of your life, there are conditions that you can attach to interactions with these people for your own safety and wellbeing.

To navigate the people – family, friends and maybe co-workers – in your life who will not accept you as autistic, you can create some unspoken basic expectations and safety rules. These are your protection barriers – your boundaries.

Who are the people you are accepting you cannot change?

. . . .

. . . .

What are your basic expectations of these people?

. . . .

. . . .

What safety rules are you going to put in place for yourself?

- What time will you choose to spend with them?
- What are the limits on this?
- Are there times or events you choose not to partic-ipate in?
- Do you want to change how you participate in events?
- Is there someone who can be a support to you when you are in this dynamic?

. . . .

. . . .

What boundaries will you put in place to accept the things you cannot change?

. . . .

. . . .

In the next chapter we'll explore finding belonging within communities and with people you share an affinity with.

This may be with the purpose of adding your voice to a movement that is demanding change or simply to share lived experiences of growing up not knowing you're autistic.

For now, note down the people and places already in your life that make you feel accepted for who you are. The people who embrace you as autistic and who you feel safe to ask questions of, to share your struggles with and to show your vulnerabilities to.

Who are the people who fully accept authentic autistic you?

. . . .

. . . .

Where are the places you feel most safe and comfortable to be autistic you?

. . . .

. . . .

What do these people and places have in common?

. . . .

. . . .

What do they offer to make you feel safe to be fully autistic you?

. . . .

. . . .

Autistic Self-Acceptance

Congratulations! You have reached a point where you accept yourself as autistic. You might have been seeking the peace that comes with self-acceptance for a lifetime.

You've worked hard to get to this point, and it deserves to be marked with acknowledgement of your breakdowns and break-throughs, and celebration that this deeper understanding and compassion will allow you to be kinder to yourself.

The benefit of you marking this milestone, by taking time to consider what you have learned and how you have grown in this process, is to record this moment for you.

This record will be something you can reflect back on, maybe as a reminder of all that you're capable of, in those tougher moments that will no doubt pop up in the future.

For learning and growing is a lifelong pursuit. There is no final destination; we continue to evolve and grow as the world does around us.

As we change our focus and output throughout our lives and we are changed by the people we come in contact with, our lives are continuously reshaped.

But there is now one major difference. You accept who you are now. You accept your strengths and your struggles, and you feel belonging – to yourself and with all the other late-discovered autists.

There is no expected timeline to get from awareness of autism to acceptance that you're autistic. It took me a couple of years. Does that mean that I am a finished article? I'm autistic! The end? No!

In writing this book, I have gone through a lot of unravelling again! I speak out and join in with many discussions about neurodivergence and that reshapes me. I am constantly learning new things about being autistic.

I know that a lot of the information I have unravelled now needs some closer attention to deepen my understanding and compassion further. I think I carry a lot of trauma from a lifetime of masking and camouflaging and only now, over three years down the line from autistic self-acceptance, am I ready to delve into that a bit deeper.

Be Kind, To Yourself... Steady, As You Go

In reaching autistic self-acceptance, what do you want to acknowledge yourself for?

. . . .

. . . .

What did you find toughest along the way? What were your breakdowns between autism awareness and autistic acceptance?

. . . .

. . . .

What or who gave you those moments of clarity? What were your breakthroughs between autism awareness and autistic acceptance?

. . . .

. . . .

What are you celebrating about *you!* What is autistic acceptance giving you?

. . . .

. . . .

What is possible for you, now and next?

. . . .

. . . .

Part 4

BELONGING

CHAPTER 13

FINDING YOUR COMMUNITY

It is a natural human instinct to find safety in belonging. To find validation in the warmth and joy of connection with another human, laughing together in the stories you share, finding inspiration and possibility in shared ideas.

It is the most natural human instinct that can be fraught with complications and difficulty for many autists.

Not all autists will struggle with friendship. You may have had an early-life supportive role model – a sibling who looked out for you and helped you to learn the ropes of friendship. Or had the luck to make an early first friend who tolerated your different ways of being and, more than that, cared for you and had your back at all times.

Some of you might have formed strong friendships with a group of people at school or university; you might all individually be, unsurprisingly, having your own late-life neurodivergent discoveries. Of course! That's why you all got on so well!

For many autists, myself included, belonging is heartbreakingly difficult.

Social communication, reading the cues and being able to have a good understanding of what others are thinking can be tricky for us. It doesn't come naturally. We have to really work at reading the cues and might never really understand what other people are thinking – especially with regards to what they think of us.

We have experienced this along with a lifetime of being rejected from friendships, groups or communities for our forthright communication and endless questioning, which is for the purpose of deeper understanding but is often mistaken for us being difficult. You might be tangled in a mighty web of Rejection Sensitivity Dysphoria (RSD).

This RSD can prevent us from even trying or finding an early exit route when our old friend anxiety triggers a flight/avoid reaction in us in relation to a friendship or group rejection.

That's why looking at belonging is an important part of this book. This is who I am... in friendship and community.

This chapter will help you to define how friendship and community matter to you. Now that you have accepted yourself as autistic, it's a good time to actively consider your way to finding belonging with individuals and groups.

Exploring this chapter and the questions within it will help you to you consider what you need from friendships to feel safe and good about yourself. We'll explore which communities are aligned with your values and what matters most to you.

Taking the time to consider this will help you to get clear on your autist's way to belonging –who you want to belong with and how.

You Belong to Me... Friendships the Disney Way

TV and film have always played an important part in my life. They are a beautiful form of escapism and an important education into how people relate to each other – how they communicate, love and laugh together.

Just as dangerous and far away from reality as the notion of Disney or fairy-tale style true love – the dashing prince rides up, saves the damsel in distress, marries her and they all live happily ever after – is the notion of Best Friends Forever (BFF).

The fantasy friendship I created in my mind from an early age was about having a best friend who I'd be close to and share secrets with without fear of them being divulged. We could talk about *anything*! We'd talk every day.

I feel that fantasy BFF notion of friendship being rammed down my throat on social media, especially on days like International Women's Day. Is it possible to get a Ya-Ya Sisterhood style friendship group when you're an autistic woman?

I had many close friendships in my life when I was growing up and I have these now. Women who I love and whose friendships I cherish. Even with those lovely friendships, I question myself... am I doing this friendship thing 'right'? Was I too annoying? Did I talk about myself too much? What do they really think of me?

I find it difficult to understand how a close friend behaves so differently when we're in larger groups. It makes me question the closeness I think I have with them.

I doubt myself. I doubt the friendship.

This can make me both anxious and avoidant as a friend.

I am inconsistent. Not exactly the right ingredients for a BFF!

This can lead me to spin off into an alternative belonging reality – estrangement. I don't feel like I belong anywhere. I feel like a total loner, a complete outsider. Nowhere more so than when I'm in a group situation, surrounded by chatty, happy people.

I often feel like I'm watching it all on a TV screen or I'm on the outside of a window looking in at this happy group and I cannot reach them.

It's the thing I struggle with the most as an autistic woman. I seek solace and fear loneliness.

Accepting myself as autistic has allowed me to start to feel belonging in different ways.

First, I've let go of the rigid notion of belonging to. When you belong to someone there is the inference of possession. A person should never belong to someone – they are not property or a possession.

Belong With

When you belong with – you're together with, a part of, have an infinity with – it feels right.

It's safe to be me and be part of this.

That's been another big shift for me since accepting myself as autistic. It's no longer about trying to fit in, to mimic and mould myself to be like you.

It is in gently finding ways to show up as me and to feel safe to have alternative thoughts and ideas that I feel like I belong.

It is in finding gentle ways to take my 'mask' off. To not feel an internal pressure to perform. To discover that yes, I am still chatty, gregarious, a storyteller and it does not require me to be at full volume to the whole room!

I prefer fewer conversations that go deeper. That's how I find belonging.

It is in finding a way to honestly say, 'I don't have the energy to come along' to this party or event. 'Thanks for asking me and keep asking me to things!'

Or 'Yes, I can come for a while.' And going along and enjoying a short time at the party and then saying, 'I've had a great time and I'm ready to go home now!'

What belonging do you want? Who with?

. . . .

. . . .

What's important to you about the people or commu-nities you belong with?

. . . .

. . . .

Friendships... the Autist's Way

What do you want from friendship? What matters most
to you about it?

. . . .

. . . .

Which friendships do you have now that you most
enjoy?

. . . .

. . . .

What are the common factors in those friendships?

. . . .

. . . .

What will help you in friendships when times are hard?

. . . .

. . . .

Communities... the Autist's Way

One of the biggest joys for me in discovering and accepting I'm
autistic is finding communities out there doing exactly the same!

Whole groups of people wanting to influence positive change
for neurodivergent people, collectively coming together and
saying, 'Your narrow views of our difference are inaccurate and
damaging. See us! Hear us! Let us in!'

It seems incredible that when I was discovering my autism in
2019/20, it was rarer to see late-discovered autistic adults sharing
their stories of late discovery than it is now.

Or maybe it's just that my autistic acceptance is aligned with my social media algorithm?!

Certainly, in the last couple of years in the UK, there have been late-discovered women with celebrity status publicly sharing their stories of late discovery. Melanie Sykes and Christine McGuinness are two of the most recent ones.

I have no doubt that many more will follow. This is a very positive thing. We need many, many more voices to join in. We need to hear more stories of late neurodivergent discovery and what it was like growing up without the information that you're neurodivergent.

It has to be better for the generations that follow us.

Autistic Social Media

I often hear the term #autistictwitter being talked about. It's in the context of autistic Twitter (X) and autistic social media in general being kind, considerate and informative.

Research carried out on autistic sociality on Twitter, published in August 2022 (Koteyko, van Driel and Vines 2022), highlighted that social media, in particular Twitter, affords autistic people affiliation strategies.

The use of hashtags allows autists to pursue interest-based conversations. The brevity of the tweet or caption enables our strength of direct communication, and there is the added benefit of it being a platform in which all small talk can be avoided!

The permanence of the records of conversations, under hashtags, allow those observing from the sidelines to gather their own research and stories about situations similar to theirs. It also allows us to scale up our voices through shared reciprocal experiences.

Furthermore, the hashtag #askingautistics provides a shortcut to the social cue that you are invited to this conversation... if you are autistic! This creates our own form of belonging.

The use of likes, retweets and follows can all be interpreted as affiliation and influence on relationship formation – evidence-based social cues.

I find emojis an excellent way to express my emotions. I have saved hours, if not days, of my life by not having to craft replies to messages! The introduction of emoji responses to acknowledge WhatsApp messages – surely that was designed by an autist?!

Reading stories or observing conversations on autistic social media formed a very large part of the early stages of my autism discovery.

In the beginning I would message directly someone who had done a post about their autism to ask them a question – to clarify what something meant.

Their responses were always warm, reassuring and informative. This helped me to take that next step into my own autism discovery.

Many of my social media direct message conversations have led to really life-affirming further exchanges.

One in particular with Rebecca Caution, who is a Coach for high masking neurodivergent adults and young people, led to some lovely Zoom interactions where we shared our stories of discovery with humour and joy at same but different challenges.

We talked openly, without judgement, with a whole lot of swearing, about how hard we find it to be parents, small talk with other parents... the hell of the playground and play dates!

I'm unlikely to meet Rebecca, in real life (IRL) but I think of her fondly and I cheer her on in her work from the sidelines. We exchange an email now and again. I shout 'Well done!' in the form of an email in response to her newsletters or to tell her of places I see her recommended for her breathwork.

I don't worry if I am an acquaintance, colleague or friend. It doesn't need to be labelled. We have shared our challenges of being late-discovered autists; that's a shared connection. This is an autist's way of belonging that works for me.

Modern-day, autist pen pals!

Inspirational Communities... the Autist's Way

What's important to you about the communities you belong to?

. . . .

. . . .

What interests do you want to share with a community? What do you want to learn or contribute to?

. . . .

. . . .

What values does the community need to have for you to feel aligned with it?

. . . .

. . . .

Changing the Conversation around Autism – a Call to Action

If you are drawn to add your voice to the ever-growing neuro-divergent communities or even to create your own community, the following activity will help you to get clear on what changes you want to see for autists and how you might become active in making those changes happen.

YOUR CALL TO ACTION CUE CARD

How do you want the conversation about autism to change?

. . . .

. . . .

. . . .

. . . .

. . . .

. . . .

What's the headline of this conversation?

. . . .

. . . .

. . . .

. . . .

. . . .

. . . .

What's the call to action of this conversation?

. . . .

. . . .

. . . .

. . . .

. . . .

. . . .

. . . .

Finding Your Community

What groups are having the conversation you want to be part of?

· ·

· ·

What activity is happening that's aligned with the changes you want to see happening?

· ·

· ·

TAKE ACTION!

Ready to be the change you want to see? Here are five actions you can take today:

1. Contact the people within the community who are having this conversation. Ask them a question or tell them your thoughts and ideas.
2. Ask how you can join in.
3. Post comments on a conversation thread.
4. Write an article about this topic and post it on social media.
5. Start a blog about this topic – engage others in this conversation and invite opinion and action.

START YOUR *OWN* COMMUNITY

If the conversation you want to have about the change you want to see is not happening, it's time for you to start it! Below is a suggested approach and prompts to help you to consider the best way for you to go about this.

Plan

1. Who do you want to invite to this conversation?
2. Where/how do you want this conversation to take place?
3. What's the purpose of this conversation/community?
4. What do you want from participants?
5. What are you inviting people to do?

Action

1. Make contact with the people you want to join you.
2. Post about it on social media/autism forums.
3. Write an article that will appear where the people you want to attract to your community will see it.
4. Gather people together – get the action started together.

Here are some things you can consider when bringing people with a common purpose together and some questions you can ask together in the forming stage.

Mission

What do we want the mission of our community to be? What do we want people to get from being part of this community? How far-reaching do we want the change to be?

Message

What change do we want to see? What values do we want to be known for? What legacy do we want to create in the change we are trying to drive?

Method

How do we want to gather people together in our community? Depending on the reach we want our change to extend to, how does our community meet up? Virtually or in person? How can we galvanize a community to become a movement?

Milestones

What will be the key things we want to achieve in the creation of this community. What will be the milestones to your collective achievements along the way?

I know that exploring belonging can be hard to do. It can bring sadness to the surface. A lifetime of yearning to be included, to be seen as 'one of the gang' and not ever feeling fully included within a group that feels safe can create deep wounds that are hidden from the world.

As an autist, knowing how to belong with a group of people can seem like an impossible mystery to solve. A lifetime of puzzling over the 'friendship game' that seems to keep you consigned to planet loner is deeply troublesome. I spent too much of my life there, and it took me to some dark places in my mind.

I wish I could go back to my younger self, living in those troublesome times, and reassure her that it will be okay. I'd say, 'There's nothing wrong with you, you are not a weirdo! You feel things so deeply; emotions can feel huge and complicated. One day you will learn who you really are and you won't have to spend enormous amounts of energy being who you think others want you to be. Authentic you will find friendship a lot easier.'

Belonging is first about you belonging to yourself. You've discovered and accepted what it is that makes you different and why this seemingly simple and straightforward thing – belonging – can be so difficult.

That's a huge step forward for you and it will help you enormously in belonging.

If you've taken the time to explore the questions and activities in this chapter, to identify what friendship and community mean to you as an autist, I hope it helps you to take your belonging to new and interesting places.

If you've started to consider how you want to show up in communities and how you want to change the conversation about autism – to change perceptions and how we're welcomed in and included as autists – keep going!

We need to keep joining our voices together... 'This is what autism sounds like, looks like, and your limited views need to change!'

If you're not there – not ready to think about what

conversations you want to join in with or changes you want to see – that is all good. Exploring what autism means for you and letting it play out in your mind is a hugely valuable exercise.

CHAPTER 14

EQUIPPED TO
SELF-ADVOCATE

Once you start to consider yourself to be autistic, or have family members who are autistic, you become aware of the terrible mistreatment of autistic people.

A large part of being equipped to advocate for yourself and your family and to speak up on behalf of the autism community is understanding the mistreatment of autistic people that is happening. This ranges from the seemingly innocuous labels we are given to the truly shocking treatment and abuse that autistic people are subjected to, particularly in the mental health sector.

The lack of education and understanding of decision makers and those on the front line in health, education and law is shocking. Not only is it shocking, it is putting the lives of autistic humans in danger.

This chapter looks to illuminate the challenges and implications of the lack of research, knowledge and neurodivergence representation in areas that affect autistic lives. This includes the often unhelpful and damaging deficit-based labels that are given to the neurodivergent community.

The aim of this is to inform you about what goes beyond prejudice and inequity, and to arm with you the knowledge you need as you consider yourself, autism and what positive change you may choose to advocate.

It is not designed to frighten you! Or to make you turn away from you considering yourself to be autistic. Understanding how autism affects you, what it gives you personally, in strengths and needs, and how you could be mistreated as a result of being autistic is all part of moving towards acceptance of being autistic.

As you move from awareness to acceptance that you're autistic, you will realize that these labels and barriers to things such as healthcare could indeed affect the quality of your life. They may already be doing so, simply because you have a curious mind that wants answers to what you consider to be straightforward questions.

When I initially started writing this chapter, the title of it was 'WTF is Mild Autism?!' It started out as a fairly innocuous rant about the ridiculousness of the labels that are applied to autistic people. I was questioning who made these decisions. I have included some of those enquiries in here; it's still relevant to illuminate them.

The evolution of my understanding and knowledge is reflected here. In moving towards my autistic acceptance I become better informed, and I can see the dangers of the labels and mistreatment of autistic folk.

The chapter also looks at the clash of the pathological and neurodiversity paradigms that we are experiencing right now. As with all change, there are difficult parts, and it feels like a fight between two opposing views. I hope that this is all part of our development and recognition as a community and that neurodiversity and social models of disability lead the way. There's still long way to go!

This book is about getting from awareness to acceptance of your late-discovered autism, and a large part of that is recording and reflecting on your thoughts, emotions and questions as you go through this process.

There are questions and activities within this chapter to encourage you to do exactly that.

One Year into Discovery...

As I was coming to terms with my autism, in awareness but not yet acceptance, at times I felt anger. At times I didn't know how I felt, couldn't put a name to it.

Writing is always a great way for me to make sense of my feelings.

In my coaching I work with people to process stuckness – to create more space for newness. Some of this can be caused by stuck emotions. We use movement, powerful questions, metaphors and visual references to make sense of this stuckness.

As well as using these tools to help the people I work with, I find them useful as ways to make sense of my own feelings.

Alexithymia is the clinical term used for problems with feeling emotion or, as the Greek meaning would have it, 'no words for emotions'. It doesn't mean you don't feel; it means you have problems putting it into words, describing it.

I wrote the following text a year after my own autism discovery in response to seeing different terms for autism and the constantly evolving terms and measures used in articles.

The labelling of and insistence on finding new ways to measure how autistic you are, by researchers and psychologists, is a real challenge for autistic folk.

As we struggle to access information and support, particularly in health and education, as we struggle to be understood and included in systems that are stacked against us and excluding huge proportions of autistic children from mainstream education, you have to wonder who these labels are for and who they are benefiting.

The autistic community is a very supportive one, and collectively our voices are challenging this constant and at times contentious desire to label us and study our genetics.

Until systems are changed to include and support neurological difference, we will need to continue to unite our voices to question the ethics and motivations of these ever-evolving labels.

WTF IS MILD AUTISM?

February 2021

'I'm sorry, I can't come to your party, I have mild autism!'

More and more I have been seeing the term mild autism in the media. What the fuck is mild autism???

The more I think about it, the more I am more than mildly pissed off at this ridiculous label and ridiculous kind of measurement put against something that we all need to be better informed about.

Not only that, mild is such an insipid word. It's right up there with pleasant isn't it? And terribly quaint and conservative England. 'What pleasant weather, so mild for the time of year' or some other such nonsensical pleasantry that fills so many ridiculous social exchanges.

I was diagnosed with autism (not the mild variety, just plain old, straight-up autism) at the end of 2020.

I have read a LOT of books and articles to understand autism and how it lives in me. In this short time of my reading, research and assessment with a clinical psychologist I have come across many different labels and measurements for autism and I don't think any of them are helpful to people who are either allistic (those who do not have autism), or on those on the autistic spectrum.

Autism Definitions

Here are some of the autism definitions that frequently appear in my reading:

Asperger Syndrome

Hans Asperger was a paediatrician in Austria. He carried out his research into autism (he didn't refer to it as that at the time) in the late 1930s and throughout the Second World War.

His work was discovered by Lorna Wing in 1981. It was

Lorna who coined the term 'Asperger Syndrome', named after his research.

Whilst there is no doubt that his research has been valuable in our understanding of how autism can present, predominately in white male children, his work was carried out for the Nazi regime for sinister motivations and with deadly consequences for those who were included in his studies. An eight-year study into his relationship with the Nazi regime published in 2018 concluded that he assisted in its euthanasia programme (Czech 2018).

Whilst Asperger was not a member of the Nazi party, he was a member of many groups affiliated with the Nazi regime.

It is documented that throughout the course of his work during the Second World War, Asperger referred children to a eugenics facility in Vienna where 800 children were killed.

The term Asperger Syndrome was used to diagnose many, mostly white males between 1994 and 2013. The term Asperger Syndrome is no longer used in diagnosis or widely used across the autism community.

ASD = Autistic Spectrum Disorder

Disorder... just let that settle for a moment, if you will. Does anyone want a label that describes their brain as disordered? No!

The spectrum element of this definition refers to the wide range of ways that autism can be experienced. Remember, when you've met one person with autism, you've met one person with autism!

Just like allistic people, each and every person with autism is unique, and their experience of autism will be unique to them.

High Functioning Autism

In essence, this definition works in the same way as the ridiculous 'mild' autism. It means that someone doesn't have any learning difficulties and can live independently, despite the neurotypical world being challenging to understand, communicate in and process.

ASC = Autistic Spectrum Condition

Ah we've moved on from 'disorder', hurray! And fair enough, 'condition' is slightly more palatable, but still, do we have an Allistic Spectrum Condition? No, I thought not!

Mild Autism

A person with 'mild autism' may have advanced communication skills and academic abilities but have very delayed social skills, severe sensory issues and/or extreme difficulties with organizational skills. The emphasis in every part of this description is deficit based.

A Note on the Word 'Symptoms'

'Symptoms' means a feature that is regarded as indicating a condition of disease or the existence of something that is undesirable.

You can see how I feel about 'disorder', so imagine the impact of having aspects of my connection with my world and the people in it described as 'symptoms'.

What reactions do you have to autism labels?

. . . .

. . . .

A Deeper Understanding of What Influences Autism Labels
The Pathology Paradigm

Pathology is the study of disease, a medical condition or a social, mental or language problem.

It's a medicalized model of disorders or conditions and it

always uses deficit-based language – it talks about what is missing or what is wrong.

When you are using this as an approach to describe differences in humans, it immediately turns that difference into a disadvantage or wrongness.

In trying to understand why pathology is used to describe autism, as I could see that this approach is having some terrible outcomes for autistic humans, I stumbled across the work of Dr Nick Walker PhD.

An article she wrote in 2016 about this very subject helped me to see what was creating the problem and the tension for autistic and neurodivergent people trying to be accepted as they are, not fixed or excluded (Walker 2023).

Reading this article about autism and the pathology paradigm brought together a lot of threads I'd been reading about how marginalized groups are oppressed by the use of deficit-based language to make them think there is something defective about them, thus marginalizing and oppressing them further.

With the pathology paradigm, there is an unequal social construction rooted in cultural norms which takes away social power from those different to the norm. There is a cultural value judgement that is at play rather than anything that is scientifically objective.

Dr Nick Walker highlights that these frameworks have been used to give an aura of scientific legitimacy to the oppression of women, indigenous people, people of colour and the Queer community.

She reminds us that homosexuality was framed as a mental disorder in the *Diagnostic and Statistical Manual of Mental Disorders* (DSM) as late as the 1970s.

It is also through the pathology paradigm that mistreatment and abuse of autistic people is allowed to happen in the name of 'therapy'.

If autism is viewed through this pathology paradigm – as a medical disorder that needs to be 'fixed' – then it legitimizes the terrible treatment that happens through Applied Behaviour Analysis (ABA), a form of therapy that aims to make autistic people behave in more neurotypical ways – and which has come in for huge amounts of criticism from the autistic community for the trauma it has caused.

The pathology paradigm is aligned with the medical model of disability. It attributes the individual's disability to medical defects, labelling them defective because of their personal deficiency – thus marginalizing and oppressing them further.

What are your thoughts on the pathology paradigm?

....

....

The Neurodiversity Paradigm

This paradigm seeks to accept the diversity of all human minds – the variation that exists in neurocognitive functioning.

When Judy Singer coined the phrase 'neurodiversity' in the 1990s, she built on work that was being developed by an autistic advocacy movement. This work continues to be shaped and developed by the community within the neurodiversity movement.

In the social dynamics at play in this paradigm, it's about accepting all of us as a form of human diversity. The neurodiversity paradigm wants to remove the dynamics of oppression and the systemic social power inequalities – these are the things that also exist in racial, gender and sexual orientation marginalization.

The neurodiversity paradigm is aligned with the social model of disability, which recognizes that a person may be disabled because of failures to accommodate them or societal and systemic barriers that conflict with traits that are not typical or that diverge from the norm.

What are your thoughts on the neurodiversity paradigm?

. . . .

. . . .

The Clash of the Paradigms

I can see how there is much friction between those who have a preference for the pathology paradigm and those who have a preference for the neurodiversity paradigm.

Preference is too soft a word – I think opposing stances is the clash we so often see.

Health, education and law institutions are currently taking a heavy pathology paradigm stance, and this is very much affecting their treatment of the neurodivergent community.

The autistic and neurodivergent community, with more and more of us having late-life discoveries, are joining our voices and seeking acceptance, systemic change and a human diversity approach to removing the barriers that can disable us.

We want the neurodiversity paradigm to drive change, and we are being met with those who seek to oppress us further with the pathology paradigm by making us seem broken.

You see it appearing more and more in mainstream media with headlines proclaiming, 'Self-diagnosis through TikTok has to stop!'

'We can't afford to deal with your demands!' they say. And of course they can't, when they are hell-bent on sticking to the medical model of disability that sees those with deficits as a burden to society!

See Chapter 11 for more on ableism.

> **What are your hopes for the neurodiversity paradigm?**
>
> . . . .
>
> . . . .

It can be really hard to absorb the realities of the mistreatment of a marginalized group of people, which may now include you or members of your family.

As with all mistreatment of groups, those at the intersections of disadvantage in gender, race, culture and class are most badly affected.

Do what you need to create some space to process this and to prevent it occupying all your mind with weight and hopelessness.

The following activities, if you feel drawn to them now or later on, are designed to help you to make sense of your feelings about this and start thinking about any part you might want to play in changing the way things are.

Draw It Out!

A large part of getting from awareness to acceptance of being autistic is to make sense of your thoughts and feelings.

The first activity lets you can try a different way of expressing what is emerging for you as you become aware of how autistic people are labelled and mistreated.

A common trait amongst autistic folk is our curiosity and thirst for knowledge. I have no doubt that you will already have carried out extensive research into autism or, if you haven't, you will start doing so when you feel ready to learn more!

As you move from awareness to acceptance of being autistic, you may want to start to get more active in commenting in or joining in with conversations. The second activity invites you to deepen your learning in action. These first actions are just about deepening your learning, not joining in... yet!

GETTING UNSTUCK – FEELINGS THAT HAVE NO WORDS

If you struggle to put your feelings into words, which is called alexithymia, have a go at finding a different way to express some feelings that may be bubbling up.

When you read about the mistreatment of autistic people, what is the thing that you are you most struggling to put into words?

In the space below, experiment with ways to express this thing – this feeling without words.

- What would it look like if you drew it?
- What colour is it?
- What texture is it?

What's the first word that pops into your head that sums up what you see in your drawing or expression about mistreatment of autistic people? Make it up if it doesn't exist!

. . . .

TAKING ACTION TO DEEPEN YOUR LEARNING

What three actions will you take towards deepening your learning within the autism community about labels, paradigms (pathology and neurodiversity) and other harmful barriers to autistic people?

1. ....
....
....
....
....

2. ....
....
....
....
....

3. ....
....
....
....
....

CHAPTER 15

BE THE CHANGE YOU WANT TO SEE

In this final chapter we will focus on the changes that you want to be put in place for autistic and neurodivergent people.

If I have not yet managed to convince you that change is required for autistic folk, let me try one more, final, time!

The quality of autistic lives is drastically affected by the trauma of a lifetime of being told we are wrong, difficult or needy. Too often, autists are rejected from all parts of society – from our first experience in education, where we are likely to be deemed difficult because of our non-compliance, our curiosity and questioning or the meltdowns caused by overwhelm and dysregulation.

Then we struggle to get any information or support from healthcare systems that focus on the symptom not the cause and focus on body parts in silos, with very little attention given to what's going on inside our heads – how our brains are wired.

These healthcare systems are dangerously ill-informed about neurodivergence and how it can present, about the struggles we experience in trying to cope and about how this affects our mental and physical wellbeing.

If as a child you are rejected from education, the damage to your self-esteem follows you for the rest of your life. The campaigning organization Ambitious about Austism (n.d.) has found that exclusions for autistic children are increasing sharply (up by 60% across England in five years, compared with a 4% increase across the total pupil population).

This exclusion from education will undoubtedly affect your future employment potential. Only 22 per cent of autistic adults are employed, and some research suggests that unemployment and underemployment for autistic adults may be as high as 85 per cent (Dunne 2022).

If your self-esteem is not damaged by the education system, then your failing health can affect your ability to work.

It's no coincidence that it's estimated that 24 per cent of male adults in prison screen positive ADHD (Young and Thome 2011), compared with 5 per cent of the overall population.

This is a heavy burden for the neurodivergent population to carry. Tragically, autistic adults who do not have a learning disability are nine times more likely than the general population to die by suicide (Autistica n.d.).

Together We Rise!

Here's the good news: together we rise! Whether via social media, newspapers, documentaries or books, our stories are being shared. We late-discovered autists and neurodivergent folk are accessing information about our own potential neurodivergence through stories from a wide variety of sources.

We still need to hear more stories from those who are marginalized at the intersections of race, sexuality, gender or age.

We can only do that by understanding that it is a privilege to disclose your neurodivergence and that psychological safety is an essential ingredient in being able to make this disclosure.

We must make safe spaces for all the voices and all the experiences of late discovery to be shared and amplified – for representation of all the autistic population.

For too long we've been shrouded in shame and carried the burden of adapting to fit to a world that has not been designed for us. We've been denied access to information about our own individual neurological difference. We've been 'wronged', oppressed and marginalized for experiencing and connecting with the world in different ways.

The Future Is Neurodivergent!

Guess what? The future is neurodivergent! With the plethora of crises caused by humans, planet earth is crying out for alternative thinkers to help us to see things differently. To work in different ways, we need alternative insight and an unconventional approach to the complex problems we are facing.

Some organizations are cottoning on to this – understanding that alternative thinkers can help them to succeed in their missions.

Neither the individual nor the organization/institution will benefit from us alternative thinkers unless our 'spiky profile' alternative needs are accommodated.

Green Shoots

Take comfort in the fact that change is already happening. When the patriarchy tries to diminish our relevance, as it often does in mainstream media by trying to discredit our existence, you know you are onto something!

I recently took part in a discussion to review an autism strategy being developed for the city I live in. The specific discussion I took part in centred on what autistic adults need to thrive in our city. The streams it considered included neuro-inclusive assessments, access to healthcare, including mental health support, and housing issues.

It was a positive experience to be in a room with other late-discovered autists. We were able to openly share our trauma of a lifetime of being made to feel 'wrong'. We instantly found synergy in sharing the effects of this on our health and what it means for us to be carrying the burden of advocating for ourselves and our families – constantly educating health and education providers and fighting for better quality of life.

Am I confident that our ideas will implemented? No! I am, however, confident that the city I live in is starting to see neurodivergence differently. That there is even the development of an autism strategy for autistic adults is something to be hopeful about. Not only that, but the person who led our discussion also has an active part in shaping the strategy, and they are a mightily astute autistic person!

Where Do I Start? We Need to Change Everything!

If, like me, you have an autist brain hell-bent on seeing the patterns, connections and systemic relationships, you immediately see inefficiencies in how things operate!

You may be persistent in getting to the crux of the matter and want the whole system to work well, not just a small insignificant part. If that's how you think, then the changes required can seem so huge and insurmountable that you may feel instantly defeated!

We may not see the changes we want to be in place for neurodivergent equity and inclusion in our lifetimes.

If we want it to be better for the people who come after us, then we must start to make positive changes happen, no matter how small that first step might be.

We all start to make positive change the very first time that we advocate for ourselves or our families. When we assert, 'No, that will not work,' or 'This is a real challenge for me and I need a change to be made to support my needs to function well,' we are taking steps towards positive change.

Joining your voice together with a group or collective that you are drawn to will give further momentum to positive change. You might have identified those groups or communities in Chapter 13.

In this final chapter the emphasis is on you having space to consider how you want the future to look and feel for yourself and other autists.

It's my final rallying call to action! A call for you to think about what you want for yourself in the future – how the quality of your life might improve when you can be the change you want to see.

Not all change needs to be implemented and acted upon immediately! Your priority, right now, may be to focus on your own healing from the discovery and acceptance of being autistic later in your life. This in itself is a mighty positive change.

The following activity allows you to capture your hopes for

the future. In writing it down, a seed may be planted that can take its own sweet time to grow – as you yourself continue to grow.

I invite you, one last time, to use this space to suspend your disbelief about things ever getting better and to allow your imagination to run free.

The following sections aim to nudge your imagination with questions that shift your perspective on what is possible.

It all has to start with making space for your hopes and dreams of a better future – a wish list. My wish list looks something like this:

Health	Education	Law
Mandatory front-line and policy-maker training in neurodivergence and how it presents across genders, culture and class		
Research into autism in women, non-binary people, people of colour		
Neuro-inclusive assessments (a neurodivergent assessment that looks at all neurodivergent traits at the same time)	50 percent of policy-makers and SEND workers are neurodivergent	
Access to neurodivergent mental health support for *all* identifying as neurodivergent	Neuro-inclusive teaching methods	
Overhaul mental health system		
Neuro-inclusive designed environments		
Social model of disability used to design new environments and inform policy/law		

YOUR WISH LIST

A VISIT TO THE FUTURE...

Grab a blank piece of paper and a pen, and follow the instructions below. Let your imagination run wild, and always trust the first thing that pops into your head – your instincts are always right!

- Point to the future – which direction are you pointing in?
- Walk in the direction you pointed to.
- What date is it in this future place?
- Where are you?
- What do you imagine going on around you?
- What's different in this future?
- What's the biggest change that created this future?

A LETTER FROM YOUR FUTURE SELF

Write a letter from your future self.

- What date is it?
- How old will you be on this future date?
- What do you want to say thank you to yourself for?
- What are you most grateful for?
- What is happening in your life at this future time?
- What is happening in the world at this future time?
- What's changed for you?
- What's changed for autistic people?
- What part did you play in that change for autists?

Well, that's it... I wrote a book! I wrote this book for *you*.

I wrote it to help you make sense of your late-life autism discovery. I wrote it for you to make sense of what might be happening for someone you love who is going through a late-life autism discovery.

I want to acknowledge you for taking the time to explore what autism means for you. For having the courage to be with discomfort in considering painful things in life or aspects of your life that you find difficult. I acknowledge you for considering new perspectives and possibilities for how you show up in the world.

I really hope this book has helped to go beyond making sense of you and autism. I hope it's helped you to remember who you are and to reclaim your strengths and see them in a new light.

I hope it's helped you to learn what you struggle with and why, to be compassionate to yourself in this new self-understanding and to take good care of yourself.

When you feel ready, I hope this book or this process helps you to find your voice and to share your truth with people who deserve to have you in their lives.

I celebrate *you* – for daring to be different! For allowing yourself to welcome neurodiversity into your life and perhaps that of your family.

Any positive change you make, from advocating for yourself or your family to speaking out about the changes you want to see, will make a difference.

I hope you find your autist's way to belonging. See you there!

READING AND RESOURCES

Read
Books

- Camouflage: The Hidden Lives of Autistic Women, Dr Sarah Bargiela
- The Artist's Way: A Spiritual Path to Higher Creativity, Julia Cameron
- The Art of Forgiveness, Lovingkindness and Peace, Jack Kornfield
- Burnt Out: The Exhausted Person's Six-Step Guide to Thriving in a Fast-Paced World, Selina Barker
- This Book is Anti Racist, Tiffany Jewell
- The Electricity of Every Living Thing: A Woman's Walk in the Wild to Find Her Way Home, Katherine May
- *Thumbsucker*, Eliza Fricker

Articles

- '"Diagnosis is rebirth": women who found out they were autistic as adults' *The Guardian*, Amelia Hill, 19 November 2021
- '"I recognised myself for the first time": the adults finally diagnosed as autistic' *The Guardian*, Amelia Hill, 31 July 2023
- 'Autistic burnout is more than burnout': https://autistic scienceperson.com/2021/09/26/autistic-burnout-is-more-than-burnout

- 'Autism and pathology', Dr Nick Walker: https://neuro queer.com/autism-and-the-pathology-paradigm

Listen
Podcasts

- 'The Late Discovered Club' with Catherine Asta
- 'The Squarepeg Podcast' with Amy Richards
- 'Call Me Disabled' with Poppy Field
- 'The Bendy Bodies Podcast' with Linda Bluestein, episode 47 – exploring the link between joint hypermobility and neurodiversity with Jessica Eccles
- 'How We Live Now' with Katherine May
- 'Room 5, Medical Mysteries' with Helena Merriman, Series 2 Episode 1: Holly Smale

Watch

- 'Locked Away: Our Autism Scandal' Dispatches, Channel 4
- 'Inside our Autistic Minds' with Chris Packham, BBC
- 'Christine McGuinness: Unmasking my Autism' BBC
- 'The Reason I Jump' directed by Jerry Rothwell, 2021
- 'Too Autistic For Black' directed by Talisha 'Tee Cee' Johnson, 2022, Warner Bros

Explore

- Genius Within, a social enterprise to help neurominorities unlock their talents: www.geniuswithin.org
- Employment Autism: www.employmentautism.org.uk
- Diversity and Ability, a social enterprise led by and for disabled people; supporting individuals, organizations and social justice projects: www.diversityandability.com
- Black SEN Mamas UK, a hub of information, advocacy and

mental health support for the community of black mothers and sole carers of SEND/neurodiverse children: www.instagram.com/blacksenmamas_uk

- National Autistic Society, a UK charity for autistic people and families: www.autism.org.uk
- Ambitious about Autism, a UK charity for autistic people and young people: www.ambitiousaboutautism.org.uk
- Autistic Girls Network, a UK charity for autistic girls that supports, educates and brings about positive change: www.autisticgirlsnetwork.org (see the excellent publication about internal presentation of autism, *Autism, Girls & Keeping it All Inside*, www.autisticgirlsnetwork.org/wp-content/uploads/2022/11/Keeping-it-all-inside.pdf)
- Autistica, a charity that funds campaigns for research into autism: www.autistica.org.uk
- Theo Smith's weekly newsletter on LinkedIn, 'Theo's Friday ND Roundup', a great newsletter about what's happening in the neurodiverse/business community: www.linkedin.com/newsletters/theo-s-friday-nd-roundup-6866040203660820480 and a weekly virtual meet up with Dr Amanda Kirby and guests: ND Teatime
- Praveen Kolluguri, neurodivergent chain breaker's biweekly newsletter on LinkedIn is informative and thought-provoking: www.linkedin.com/in/praveen-kolluguri
- The Autism & Neurodiversity Masterclass: https://autismmasterclass.com

Support

- Thriving Autistic, a global team of neurodivergent psychologists, coaches and practitioners: www.thrivingautistic.org

Neuro-Inclusive Assessments

- The Adult Autism Practice: www.adultautism.ie
- Divergent Life: www.divergentlife.co.uk

REFERENCES

Alexander, J. (2020) 'A time for Citizens.' Medium. https://jonjalex.medium.com/a-time-for-citizens-2c15f542a449.

Ambitious about Autism (n.d.) 'Exclusions.' https://www.ambitiousaboutautism.org.uk/what-we-do/policy-and-campaigns/campaigns/education/exclusions.

Autistica (n.d.) 'Suicide and autism.' www.autistica.org.uk/what-is-autism/signs-and-symptoms/suicide-and-autism.

Baron-Cohen, S., Wheelwright, S., Skinner, R., Martin, J. and Clubley, E. (2001) 'The autism-spectrum quotient (AQ): Evidence from Asperger syndrome/high-functioning autism, males and females, scientists and mathematicians.' *Journal of Autism and Developmental Disorders 31*, 1, 5–17.

Cage, E. and Troxell-Whitman, Z. (2019) 'Understanding the Reasons, Contexts and Costs of Camouflaging for Autistic Adults.' *Journal of Autism and Developmental Disorders 49*, 1899–1911.

Cassidy, S. A., Gould, K., Townsend, E., Pelton, M., Robertson, A. E. and Rodgers, J. (2019) 'Is Camouflaging Autistic Traits Associated with Suicidal Thoughts and Behaviours? Expanding the Interpersonal Psychological Theory of Suicide in an Undergraduate Student Sample.' *Journal of Autism and Developmental Disorders 50*, 10, 3638–3648.

Czech, H. (2018) 'Hans Asperger, National Socialism, and "race hygiene" in Nazi-era Vienna.' *Molecular Autism 9*, 29.

Dunne, M. (2022) 'What workplace model best suits neurodiverse employees?' CIPD. www.peoplemanagement.co.uk/article/1804949/workplace-model-best-suits-neurodiverse-employees.

Koteyko, N., van Driel, M. and Vines, J. (2022) 'Autistic sociality on Twitter: Enacted affordances and affiliation strategies.' *Discourse & Communication 16*, 4, 385–402.

Lord, C., Rutter, M. and Le Couteur, A. (1994) 'Autism Diagnostic Interview-Revised: A revised version of a diagnostic interview for caregivers of individuals with possible pervasive developmental disorders. *Journal of Autism and Developmental Disorders 24*, 5, 659–685.

Price, D. (2023a) [Instagram post] www.instagram.com/reel/CoDWvflMtci.

Price, D. (2023b) [Instagram post] www.instagram.com/reel/CoDXL9VOQMl/?igshid=MDJmNzVkMjY%3D.

Raymaker, D. (2022) 'Understanding autistic burnout.' National Autistic Society. www.autism.org.uk/advice-and-guidance/professional-practice/autistic-burnout.

Walker, N. (2023) 'Autism & the pathology paradigm.' https://neuroqueer.com/autism-and-the-pathology-paradigm.

Young, S. and Thome, J. (2011) 'ADHD and offenders.' *The World Journal of Biological Psychiatry12*, 1, 124–128.